Winning Bridge

Winning Bridge

VICTOR MOLLO

BEAUFORT BOOKS, INC.
New York

Library of Congress Cataloging in Publication Data

Mollo, Victor.
Winning bridge.

1. Contract bridge.   I. Title.
GV1282.3.M593   1984   795.41′5   84-9312
ISBN 0-8253-0234-X

Published in the United States by Beaufort Books, Inc., New York.

Printed in the U.S.A.   First American Edition

10 9 8 7 6 5 4 3 2 1

Contents

Author's Preface

Neither a textbook, nor a quiz book, *Winning Bridge* has some of the characteristics of both. The purpose behind it is to entertain and to instruct. The medium is a collection of hands, each one with a message and a problem, and a challenge to the reader to solve it.

In selecting the material I have ranged far and wide, in space and in time. Some of the examples are from rubber bridge at the Eccentric, then the St James's Bridge Club, descendants in turn of famous Crockford's, for years the home of Britain's leading players and the chosen venue of distinguished visitors from overseas. Many examples are from competitive bridge, selected as the most interesting of the day by writers in bridge magazines at home and abroad. I have creamed the cream, from the best, picking the best. To impart knowledge and to tickle the reader's palate, that has always been my twin objective and it has determined the selection of every hand.

Readers of my *Evening Standard* column in days gone by may recognise some of the *dramatis personae*. The unlucky Professor, the Guardian Angel and other members of the cast are about to come once more before the footlights. They belong to my theme as does the title of the book which is taken from my erstwhile column. It's hardly original, but it happens to be my favourite pastime, and will soon be the reader's, too, I hope, if it isn't already.

In all my books, and this my computer tells me is the twenty-fourth, I have a fall guy — or should I say fall person? If there was a slip somewhere, I could blame it on a friendly expert, who had read the text and failed to spot it, or maybe on my wife, who makes sure that no hand has more than its fair share of cards or clubs or spades or sixes, tiresome details for which I show on occasion a lofty disdain.

This time I am all on my own. I have chosen every hand with cold deliberation, rejecting ninety-nine to pick the hundredth. If you don't absorb a lot of good bridge and, above all, enjoy yourself in the process, the fault will be mine and I shall have no alibi. So please, dear reader, enjoy yourself. Don't let me down.

1   *The First, Fateful Move*

On many a hand the point of no return comes at take off. The contract is makable at trick one, impossible thereafter. When dummy comes down, that's the time to think and work out the best line of play, for there may not be another chance till the post-mortem. Even dummy, *le mort* as the French say, has a part to play, or rather not to play. If he doesn't lie down soon enough, if, as some do, he helpfully flicks a singleton on the opening lead, he may prejudice declarer's chances.

Say that as he tables his hand, partner throws a bare queen on West's three or four of the suit and East covers with the king. If South stops to think, whether or not to take the trick, he will be telling East that he has the ace. Alternatively, if he hasn't, a pause could be misleading, and fearing to be unethical, South may play too quickly. No time to select a false card or to prepare to follow smoothly to the next trick. Sometimes it will make no difference. Sometimes it will.

The hands which follow in this chapter highlight the different facets of the problem which so often face declarer at trick one. Dummy should have none.

Dlr. South
N/S vul.

       ♠ Q J 5
       ♡ 5 3 2
       ◇ A J 10 9 8 7
       ♣ 2

        N
      W E
       S

       ♠ A 4 2
       ♡ A K 8 7
       ◇ K
       ♣ Q J 9 6 5

South	West	North	East
1♣	1♠	2◇	Pass
2♡	Pass	3◇	Pass
3NT			

West leads the ♣8. Can declarer ensure his contract against any distribution?

Yes, the contract is unbeatable — except by declarer himself. The key play comes at trick one.

It's true that West is likely to have the ♠K, and the 'natural' play is to go up with the ♠Q, win the trick — and lose the contract. For now there will no entry to dummy's precious diamonds.

At trick one, declarer should play low from dummy, winning with the ♠A. Next the ◇K is overtaken and the ◇Q is driven out. Whatever the return, South leads a spade.

  ♠ K 10 9 8 6   ♠ 7 3
  ♡ 6 4   N   ♡ Q J 10 9
  ◇ 4 3 2   W E ◇ Q 6 5
  ♣ A K 8   S   ♣ 10 7 4 3

The defence cannot come to more than: one diamond, one spade and two clubs.

The diagrammed hand presents an instructive variation on an old theme.

Dlr. South
Love all

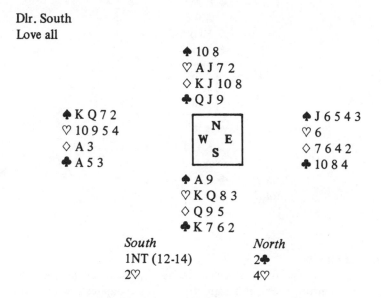

North
♠ 10 8
♡ A J 7 2
◇ K J 10 8
♣ Q J 9

West
♠ K Q 7 2
♡ 10 9 5 4
◇ A 3
♣ A 5 3

East
♠ J 6 5 4 3
♡ 6
◇ 7 6 4 2
♣ 10 8 4

South
♠ A 9
♡ K Q 8 3
◇ Q 9 5
♣ K 7 6 2

South	North
1NT (12-14)	2♣
2♡	4♡

West leads the ♠K. How should South play?

In view of the 4-1 break, which soon comes to light, declarer cannot afford to draw trumps before forcing out the ◇A and ♣A. So he leads the ◇5 and goes up with dummy's ◇K. Why? Because he wants East to play the ◇A, if he has it. After all, West could have the ◇Q.

The ◇K wins, of course, and South turns to the clubs, driving out the ♣A.

Who is going to win?

The answer depends, as it does so often, on what happened at trick one. If declarer played low, he will make his contract. If he went up with the ♠A, he won't. An alert West will play off his ◇A and underplay the ♠Q. Coming in with the ♠J, East will give his partner a diamond ruff.

Playing low at trick one is sound technique. It costs nothing, and may, as above, *sever communications between East and West*.

Dlr. South
Both vul.

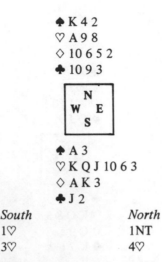

```
                    ♠ K 4 2
                    ♡ A 9 8
                    ◇ 10 6 5 2
                    ♣ 10 9 3

                       N
                    W     E
                       S

                    ♠ A 3
                    ♡ K Q J 10 6 3
                    ◇ A K 3
                    ♣ J 2
```

South	North
1♡	1NT
3♡	4♡

West leads the ♠J.

At rubber bridge or in a match the hand presents no problem, for South has ten top tricks. But suppose that it's a duplicate pairs event. The eleventh trick would make a big difference. How should South play?

A 3-3 diamond break will yield the extra trick, so long as declarer has time to develop it, before defenders switch to clubs. And, of course, they will switch at once when they realise the position in the other suits.

To keep opponents guessing, South plays low to the first trick! He wins the likely spade continuation, cashes the ◇ A K and takes two rounds of trumps, ending in dummy. After discarding the ◇3 on the ♠K, South ruffs a diamond.

```
    ♠ J 10 9 8                          ♠ Q 7 6 5
    ♡ 5 2              N                ♡ 7 4
    ◇ Q 8 7        W       E            ◇ J 9 4
    ♣ A Q 5 4          S                ♣ K 8 7 6
```

The odds are against a 3-3 diamond break, but it costs virtually nothing to try. The slight risk of a diamond ruff, before trumps are drawn, is well worth taking with match-point scoring.

The hand below came up in a Swedish tournament. Declarer went down on a contract which he should have made. Where did he slip?

Dlr. South
N/S vul.

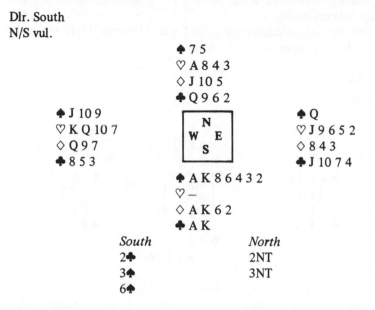

♠ 7 5
♡ A 8 4 3
◇ J 10 5
♣ Q 9 6 2

♠ J 10 9
♡ K Q 10 7
◇ Q 9 7
♣ 8 5 3

♠ Q
♡ J 9 6 5 2
◇ 8 4 3
♣ J 10 7 4

♠ A K 8 6 4 3 2
♡ –
◇ A K 6 2
♣ A K

South	North
2♣	2NT
3♠	3NT
6♠	

West led the ♡K. Winning with the ♡A, declarer was in dummy for the first and last time, so he promptly took the losing finesse in diamonds. As the trumps didn't break kindly either, he had to concede defeat.

Admittedly it was an unlucky hand, the odds being well in declarer's favour. They would have been better still had he not slipped at trick one, the usual place.

South should ruff the ♡K in hand and test the trumps. When East fails on the second round, he cashes the ♣ A K and exits with a third trump. West is helpless, for whatever he plays gives declarer access to two tricks in dummy.

If East shows up with three trumps, South cashes one top diamond and throws him in. He returns a diamond, no doubt, and the contract is no longer a certainty, but the diamond finesse hasn't run away. Meanwhile, South has doubled his chances.

One of the expert's advantages is that having confronted the same seemingly difficult situations again and again, he acquires a technique for dealing with them. It has nothing to do with flair and is largely a matter of experience.

Declarer on the diagrammed hand was Alphonse Moyse, for many years editor of America's *Bridge World*.

Dlr. West
E/W vul.

```
                        ♠ 7
                        ♡ 5 3
                        ◇ A K Q 9 3
                        ♣ Q 9 8 5 2
   ♠ K Q J 9 6 2                           ♠ 10 4
   ♡ Q 6 4              ┌──────────┐       ♡ 8 7 2
   ◇ 7 2               │    N     │       ◇ J 10 4
   ♣ A J               │  W   E   │       ♣ K 10 7 4 3
                        │    S     │
                        └──────────┘
                        ♠ A 8 5 3
                        ♡ A K J 10 9
                        ◇ 8 6 5
                        ♣ 6
```

West	North	East	South
1♠	2◇	Pass	3♡
Pass	4♡		

West leads the ♠K. How should South play?

If he wins and ruffs a spade, the defence will come to a trump, two spades and a club. If South leads the ♡J at trick two, West will win and return a second spade, and South, ruffing in dummy, won't be able to get back to draw trumps.

What's the solution?

Feeling, no doubt, 'I've been there before', Moyse allowed West to win the first trick! Another spade followed, but now Moyse could afford to ruff, retaining the ♠A intact, and draw trumps.

There are many variations on this theme when, to keep control, declarer should concede a trick to which opponents do not appear to be entitled.

Dlr. South
Love all

```
                    ♠ 5 2
                    ♡ 10 4 3
                    ◇ K J 10 9
                    ♣ K J 6 5
               ┌─────────┐
               │    N    │
               │  W   E  │
               │    S    │
               └─────────┘
                    ♠ A 4 3
                    ♡ A Q 6
                    ◇ Q 8 7
                    ♣ A Q 8 7
```

South	North
1♣	1◇
2NT	3NT

West led the ♣6 to East's ♣K. The contract was unbreakable – by the defence – but taking the 'wrong view', declarer went down.

West's lead of the ♣6 is the key. There's no reason to doubt that it's a true card, and if it is, the spades will break harmlessly 4-4, for with 5 4 3 2 on view, the 6 can only be the fourth highest of a *four-card suit*.

Declarer should, therefore, win the *first trick* and drive out the ◇A. The defence can cash three spades, but no more.

```
♠ Q 10 8 6              ♠ K J 9 7
♡ K J 7 2               ♡ 9 8 5
◇ 6 3 2                 ◇ A 5 4
♣ 10 9                  ♣ 4 3 2
```

What doubtless happened was that, obeying a reflex, declarer held up automatically his ♣A and East promptly switched to a heart. Now all is lost. If South ducks, West wins and goes back to spades. If South rises with the ♡A, he will lose three hearts when East comes in with the ◇A.

Dlr. South
Love all

```
             ♠ A 8 3
             ♡ 5 3
             ◇ Q 10 9
             ♣ A 8 7 5 3
                   N
                W     E
                   S
             ♠ K 10
             ♡ K 4
             ◇ A K J 8 7 6
             ♣ K 4 2
```

South	West	North	East
1◇	3♡	4◇	Pass
5◇			

West leads the ◇2. How should South play?

Since the ♡A is almost certainly wrong, South can see three losers — two hearts and a club. The only hope is to establish a club without losing the lead to the East.

This can be done if West has three clubs, and also if he has the bare ♣ Q J, for then declarer could allow him to hold the second trick. With ♣ Q x, West could foil this play by jettisoning the ♣Q on South's ♣K.

South can, however, give himself another chance. Winning the first trick in dummy, he leads a spade, inserting the ♠10, unless East plays an honour.

Whatever West returns, South wins, cashes the ♠K, crosses to dummy with a trump and throws a club on the ♠A. Now comes the ♣K, the ♣A and a club ruff. Two clubs are set up in dummy and a trump provides an entry.

```
♠ Q 9 6                          ♠ J 7 5 4 2
♡ A Q J 10 9 7 6      N          ♡ 8 2
◇ 2                 W   E        ◇ 5 4 3
♣ 10 9                S          ♣ Q J 6
```

All's well — so long as declarer paused to think before playing to trick one and won it in dummy.

'As usual,' said the Professor bitterly, 'every card was wrong.'
'*Seemed* to be wrong,' corrected the Senior Kibitzer.

Dlr. South
Both vul.

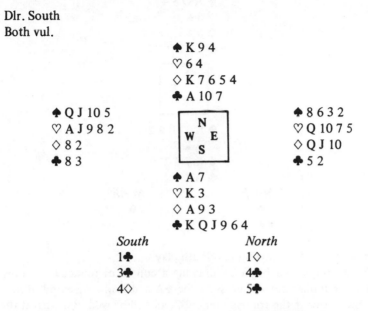

	♠ K 9 4	
	♡ 6 4	
	◇ K 7 6 5 4	
	♣ A 10 7	
♠ Q J 10 5		♠ 8 6 3 2
♡ A J 9 8 2		♡ Q 10 7 5
◇ 8 2		◇ Q J 10
♣ 8 3		♣ 5 2
	♠ A 7	
	♡ K 3	
	◇ A 9 3	
	♣ K Q J 9 6 4	

South	North
1♣	1◇
3♣	4♣
4◇	5♣

West led the ♠Q. Winning with the ♠A, the Professor took two rounds
of trumps and led a low diamond from dummy, intending to insert the
◇9, so as to keep East out of the lead.

East, however, couldn't be kept out and a heart through the closed
hand spelt declarer's doom.

'The odds against this distribution . . .' began the Professor. 'A rather
favourable distribution,' rejoined SK unkindly. 'With trumps and
diamonds breaking nicely, the odds in your favour were roughly 100
per cent.

'All you had to do was to let West hold the first trick. You win the
next one, another spade, maybe, and after drawing trumps, you throw
a diamond on dummy's ♠K. Now the ◇A, the ◇K and a diamond ruff
will set up two long diamonds for heart discards and all is well. In fact,
unless West cashes his ♡A at trick two, you should come to twelve
tricks — instead of ten.'

Dlr. South
Love all

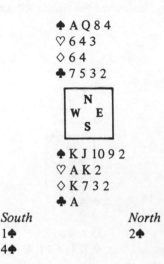

♠ A Q 8 4
♥ 6 4 3
♦ 6 4
♣ 7 5 3 2

♠ K J 10 9 2
♥ A K 2
♦ K 7 3 2
♣ A

South	North
1♠	2♠
4♠	

West leads the ♣Q. How should South play?

Most Souths will begin by drawing a couple of rounds of trumps.
The more thoughtful will cross to the ♠A and lead a diamond. If East
has the ♦A or if the trumps break 2-2, all will be well. But what if the
East-West hands are:

♠ 7 5 3   ♠ 6
♥ J 9 5   ♥ Q 10 8 7
♦ A Q 10 9   ♦ J 8 5
♣ Q J 10   ♣ K 9 8 6 4

Now West will come in twice, with the ♦A and ♦Q, and each time he
will lead a trump. Confined to one diamond ruff in dummy, South will
lose three diamonds and a heart.

Restraining the impulse to draw trumps — or to lead diamonds from
dummy — South should be thankful that he didn't get a trump lead.
Instead of doing defenders' work for them, he should lead a diamond
at once from his hand. Now no one can stop him from ruffing two
diamonds and scoring ten tricks.

Here declarer makes his first move at trick two, but the principle
is the same. Once the Rubicon is crossed it is too late to turn back.

2 *Advanced Problems in Elementary Arithmetic*

Should a computer be programmed some day to play good bridge – which I am inclined to doubt – it will be despite, not because of, its mathematical prowess. Exercises in elementary arithmetic come up on every hand. Higher mathematics never. Counting up to eight, nine or ten can be hard enough for declarer. Bringing the addition correctly to three, four or five can be harder still for defenders. Which are the certain winners, which are probable, and if so, *how* probable? It isn't easy to do sums without seeing the figures.

There is a technique for dealing with every situation, but not for identifying the situation itself. That is a matter of inference and deduction, calling for judgment and imagination.

Should defenders try to score their winners before declarer scores his? Or should they sit back, passively, hoping that, left to his own devices, declarer won't have enough for his quota?

Whichever it is, the addition is usually in single figures and can never exceed thirteen. The arithmetic is elementary. Not so the problems to which it often gives rise, as the next group of hands will show.

Dlr. South
N/S vul.

```
                        ♠ 4 3 2
                        ♡ A J 10 2
                        ◇ Q 7 6
                        ♣ K J 3
                    ┌─────────┐          ♠ J 6 5
                    │    N    │          ♡ 7 5
                    │ W     E │          ◇ A 10 9
                    │    S    │          ♣ A 9 7 6 5
                    └─────────┘
```

South	West	North	East
1♡	1♠	3♡	3♠
4♡			

West led the ♠K. Declarer won with the ♠A, drew trumps in two rounds, West discarding a spade the second time, and continued with the ♣Q. West's ♣2 indicated three clubs, and so East held up his ♣A. Another club followed and East won. What card should he play next?

East reasoned that South was unlikely to have a second spade and that on his bid West surely had the ◇K. Hoping to find him with the ◇J, as well, East switched to the ◇10, before South could discard on dummy's ♣K. That gave South his contract. Where did East go wrong?

```
          ♠ K Q 10 9 8 7
          ♡ 3                  ┌─────────┐
          ◇ K 5 2              │    N    │
          ♣ 10 8 2             │ W     E │
                               │    S    │
                               └─────────┘
                        ♠ A
                        ♡ K Q 9 8 6 4
                        ◇ J 8 4 3
                        ♣ Q 3
```

East knew of nine cards in South's hands — six trumps, the ♠A and two clubs. So he had four diamonds, conceivably three diamonds and a spade. Getting rid of one loser wouldn't help him, for he would still have only nine winners — unless West presented him with a tenth by opening up the diamonds.

Dlr. South
Love all

```
                    ♠ J 9 7
                    ♡ A K Q 7 4
                    ◇ 4 3 2
                    ♣ 5 4
                                        ♠ 10 8 3
              ┌───────────┐             ♡ 10 5 3
              │     N     │             ◇ A 10 8
              │  W     E  │             ♣ J 9 7 2
              │     S     │
              └───────────┘
```

South	West	North	East
1♣	1♠	2♡	Pass
4♣	Pass	4♡	Pass
5♣			

West leads the ♠K, then the ◇9 to East's ◇A. What should East return?

The key to the play lies in the bidding. Why didn't South pass 4♡? Clearly because he has at best a singleton heart and presumably seven clubs.

Once he sees West show out in trumps he will cross to dummy with his only heart and take the marked finesse against East's ♣J. East should, therefore, remove declarer's only link with dummy *before* the 4-0 trump split comes to light.

A diamond return is uninspired but the worst is a spade. If South could have a second spade, West would have cashed his ♠A.

Dlr. West
N/S vul.

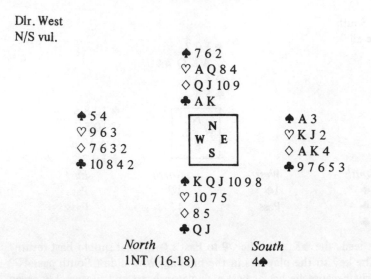

♠ 7 6 2
♡ A Q 8 4
◇ Q J 10 9
♣ A K

♠ 5 4
♡ 9 6 3
◇ 7 6 3 2
♣ 10 8 4 2

♠ A 3
♡ K J 2
◇ A K 4
♣ 9 7 6 5 3

♠ K Q J 10 9 8
♡ 10 7 5
◇ 8 5
♣ Q J

North	*South*
1NT (16-18)	4♠

West leads the ♣2. A trump to declarer's king, followed by another, puts East on play. What should he do?

Most players will take a passive line, hoping to break the contract by scoring two tricks in diamonds, and one more with the ♡K. A club return is eminently 'safe' — and fatal.

A moment's reflection will show that declarer must have six trumps, at least. That's five tricks. The ♣AK and ♡A will yield three more, and given time, he will set up two tricks in diamonds, ten tricks in all.

To beat the contract, East must develop a heart before South establishes his two diamonds. A switch to hearts, based on the hope that West has the ♡10, is therefore, imperative.

He hasn't, as it happens, but the ♡9 may do, for not every South will play the ♡10. And if he doesn't, defenders are one move ahead.

Dlr. South
E/W vul.

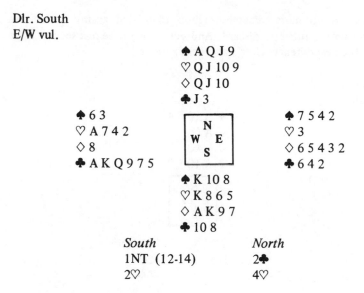

<pre>
              ♠ A Q J 9
              ♡ Q J 10 9
              ◇ Q J 10
              ♣ J 3
  ♠ 6 3   ♠ 7 5 4 2
  ♡ A 7 4 2   N   ♡ 3
  ◇ 8   W   E   ◇ 6 5 4 3 2
  ♣ A K Q 9 7 5   S   ♣ 6 4 2
              ♠ K 10 8
              ♡ K 8 6 5
              ◇ A K 9 7
              ♣ 10 8
</pre>

South	North
1NT (12-14)	2♣
2♡	4♡

West's ♣K and ♣Q won the first two tricks. East followed with the ♣2, then the ♣4, showing an odd number of clubs, clearly three, since he couldn't have five.

How should West continue?

The ◇8 would be pointless, for if East had the ◇A, the contract would be beaten anyway. A trump would be safe, but unhelpful. So West switched to a spade — and lived to regret it.

There was no room for East to have the ♠K, but even if he had it, the king wouldn't run away.

West's one asset was his length in trumps. To capitalise it, all he had to do was to continue clubs. It would present declarer with a ruff and discard, but what matter?

A third club would reduce declarer's or dummy's trumps to three. West would then hold up his ♡A until the third round. Then, when either declarer or dummy had no more trumps, he would win and lead another club, depriving South of trump control — and of the contract.

There is no more venerable taboo than that against presenting declarer with a ruff and discard. And yet, as we have just seen, it is, at times, the best defence. Here's another example:

Dlr. South
Love all

```
                    ♠ A 10 5 4
                    ♡ A Q
                    ◊ 6 4 3
                    ♣ A 10 8 7
    ♠ Q 3 2           ┌─────────┐
    ♡ J 6 2           │    N    │
    ◊ K Q J 9         │ W     E │
    ♣ J 6 5           │    S    │
                      └─────────┘
```

	South	*North*
	1NT (12-14)	2♣
	2♠	4♠

West leads the ◊K then the ◊Q. Declarer wins the second trick with the ◊A and continues with the ♡K, then the ♡4 to the ♡A. Next he exits with dummy's third diamond, all following. West counts declarer's hand, the basis of every sound defence.

South is known to have three diamonds and obviously two hearts only, otherwise he would have discarded dummy's third diamond on his ♡K. With five spades he would have probably opened 1♠ rather than 1NT. So he doubtless has four spades and four clubs.

Should West now lead the ♡J, it will violate the taboo, for South will ruff in one hand and discard from the other. A club discard, however, cannot help him. A club or trump return may well do so, if the other hands are:

```
     ┌─────────┐      ♠ J 6
     │    N    │      ♡ 10 9 8 7 5 3
     │ W     E │      ◊ 10 8 7
     │    S    │      ♣ Q 4
     └─────────┘
      ♠ K 9 8 7
      ♡ K 4
      ◊ A 5 2
      ♣ K 9 3 2
```

A feature common to several of the world's best-known bridge magazines is a quiz for experts. Tricky questions are submitted to a panel of internationals and the readers are invited to participate.

Here's a hand from the Swedish *Bridge Tidningen*.

Dlr. West
Both vul.

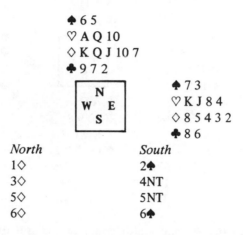

♠ 6 5
♡ A Q 10
◇ K Q J 10 7
♣ 9 7 2

♠ 7 3
♡ K J 8 4
◇ 8 5 4 3 2
♣ 8 6

North	South
1◇	2♠
3◇	4NT
5◇	5NT
6◇	6♠

West leads the ♡2. Dummy's ♡Q loses to East's ♡K, declarer following with the ♡5. Which card should East play back?

Most Easts would return a club. A few — a very few, I hope — might try a trump. Both would be wrong. South wouldn't have bid 5NT without three aces, and if he has a trump loser, he will go down anyway. Meanwhile, a club can't help for he can always discard a club loser on dummy's diamonds. The only hope is to cut him off from the table. Only three diamonds are missing, and if South's ◇A is bare his sole link with dummy is the ♡A. A heart from East, killing that entry, presents declarer with a trick in hearts, but deprives him of four tricks in diamonds.

Which side shall we back?

Dlr. West
N/S game

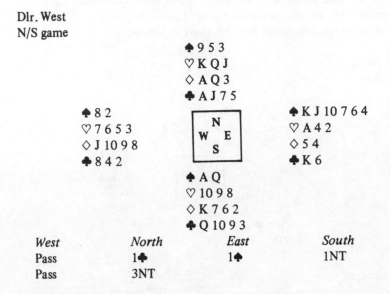

| ♠953 |
| ♡KQJ |
| ◇AQ3 |
| ♣AJ75 |

```
               ♠ 9 5 3
               ♡ K Q J
               ◇ A Q 3
               ♣ A J 7 5
  ♠ 8 2                          ♠ K J 10 7 6 4
  ♡ 7 6 5 3          N           ♡ A 4 2
  ◇ J 10 9 8      W     E        ◇ 5 4
  ♣ 8 4 2            S           ♣ K 6
               ♠ A Q
               ♡ 10 9 8
               ◇ K 7 6 2
               ♣ Q 10 9 3
```

West	North	East	South
Pass	1♣	1♠	1NT
Pass	3NT		

West led the ♠8 and South could see six top tricks — two spades, three diamonds and a club. He could set up two hearts quickly, but then his second spade stopper would go, before he could clear the clubs.

Since diamonds don't break, should we back the defence?

This is what happened. South drove out the ♡A, but expecting the club finesse to fail, in view of East's bid, he cashed his red winners, ending in dummy, and with five cards left, exited with a spade. Let East lead clubs himself.

Are we now on South's side?

Double dummy South must win. But the hand wasn't played double dummy and East could see in time what was coming. So, on the third diamond he smoothly discarded the ♣6. South was suspicious, but he couldn't tell whether East had started with six spades and two clubs or five spades and three clubs. Misguessing, he threw East in with a spade.

After a while even partner forgave him.

'Above all, not too much zeal,' Talleyrand's advice to his staff, would have stood East in good stead here:

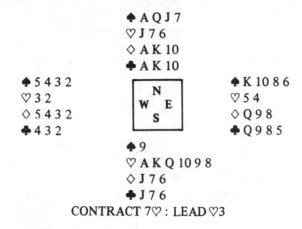

```
              ♠ A Q J 7
              ♡ J 7 6
              ◇ A K 10
              ♣ A K 10
♠ 5 4 3 2      ┌─────────┐    ♠ K 10 8 6
♡ 3 2          │    N    │    ♡ 5 4
◇ 5 4 3 2      │ W     E │    ◇ Q 9 8
♣ 4 3 2        │    S    │    ♣ Q 9 8 5
              └─────────┘
              ♠ 9
              ♡ A K Q 10 9 8
              ◇ J 7 6
              ♣ J 7 6
```

CONTRACT 7♡ : LEAD ♡3

The bidding is best forgotten. The contract is a wretched one, but the play is of interest.

With only eleven tricks on top, even a finesse won't suffice. Should declarer take two finesses? It would be humiliating in a grand slam and South felt he could do much better.

First he cashed the ◇A K and the ♣A K. Then he reeled off his trumps, ten tricks in all. If, in addition to the ♠K — the vital card — West also had one of the queens, he would by now be helpless.

Turn to East. Surely he was doomed. With both queens, how could he also guard his ♠K? Fortunately, South couldn't tell the position so East bared his ♠K early on without blinking.

South was about to take the spade finesse and go three down, when West came to the rescue. To help East, to give him a count, he threw all his four spades! South counted, too, and going up with the ♠A, he triumphantly brought down East's lone ♠K.

Dlr. East
Love all

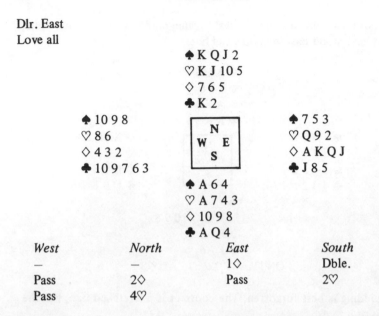

                    ♠ K Q J 2
                    ♡ K J 10 5
                    ◇ 7 6 5
                    ♣ K 2

     ♠ 10 9 8   ♠ 7 5 3
     ♡ 8 6   N   ♡ Q 9 2
     ◇ 4 3 2   W   E   ◇ A K Q J
     ♣ 10 9 7 6 3   S   ♣ J 8 5

                    ♠ A 6 4
                    ♡ A 7 4 3
                    ◇ 10 9 8
                    ♣ A Q 4

West	North	East	South
—	—	1◇	Dble.
Pass	2◇	Pass	2♡
Pass	4♡		

West leads a diamond and East cashes the ◇AKQ. How should he
continue?

It is simply not possible for West to have an ace or any other high
card, for that matter, so it looks as if the only hope of setting the contract lies in winning a trick with the ♡Q. But then, just as West can
place South, on the bidding, with all the outstanding honour cards,
South can return the compliment and the ♡Q is doomed from the start.

Can East do anything about it?

There is one ray of hope. Though West can have no high cards, he
may well have an eight, and it could be the ♡8. If so, all isn't lost. East
leads his fourth diamond, presenting declarer with a ruff and discard.
It's not much of a gift for he has no loser to discard, but it allows West
to ruff with the ♡8, forcing the ♡10 (or ♡J) from dummy, and now
East has a certain trump trick.

Dlr. West
Love all

```
            ♠ 10 9 8 7
            ♡ 3 2
            ◇ K 8 6 5
            ♣ Q 10 3
                              ♠ J 2
            ┌─────────┐       ♡ K 4
            │    N    │       ◇ 9 4 3 2
            │  W   E  │       ♣ A J 9 7 6
            │    S    │
            └─────────┘
```

West	North	East	South
Pass	Pass	Pass	1♠
Dble.	2♠	3♣	4♠

West leads the ♣2 and East's ♣J wins the first trick. What card should he play next?

Since West couldn't open as dealer, but came in over South's 1♠, he is clearly short in spades and is worth about 10-11 points. His ♣2 shows four clubs. It could be three, but it's unlikely, if only because of South's jump to 4♠.

Placing West with an ace, East should lead the ♡K. If West has the ♡A, the defence will score the first four tricks, for East can over-ruff dummy. But it isn't essential for West to have the ♡A. It is enough for him to have the ♡Q and the ♠A, as happened when this hand came up at rubber bridge.

```
♠ A 3
♡ Q 7 6 5          ┌─────────┐
◇ Q 10 7           │    N    │
♣ K 8 5 2          │  W   E  │
                   │    S    │
                   └─────────┘
            ♠ K Q 6 5 4
            ♡ A J 10 9 8
            ◇ A J
            ♣ 4
```

It is true that West might have had the ◇A instead of the ♠A, but if so, no defence would have prevailed. The lead of the ♡K could gain and couldn't lose.

The trouble with being clever is that not many players have the will-power to practise it in moderation and the successes are too few to make up for the failures. A rich reward awaits those who can wait patiently for the right occasion, such as occurred in an international match reported in the Belgian magazine, *Bridge*.

Dlr. North
E/W vul.

```
                 ♠ Q 7
                 ♡ A Q 5 4 3
                 ◊ K Q 7 2
                 ♣ 6 4
   ♠ 5 4 3 2                    ♠ K J 10 9
   ♡ K 9 8        N             ♡ 10 7 6 2
   ◊ 4         W     E          ◊ A 8
   ♣ J 10 8 3 2    S            ♣ K Q 9
                 ♠ A 8 6
                 ♡ J
                 ◊ J 10 9 6 5 3
                 ♣ A 7 5
```

North	South
1♡	2◊
3◊	3NT

West led the ♣J. East overtook with the ♣Q, declarer playing low. Which card should East play?

East reasoned that, on his bidding, South was marked with the two black aces. So he would hold up his ♣A a second time and thereafter West would have no entry.

Seeing no future in clubs, East returned, not the ♣K, but the ♣9! South ducked, as expected, and West rubbed his eyes. Who had the ♣K? South wouldn't have played low twice with the ♣AK. So East had it. Why, then, didn't he play it? Clearly because he badly wanted a switch. It couldn't be hearts, so overtaking the ♣9, West switched to a spade. Curtains for South.

Dlr. West
Love all

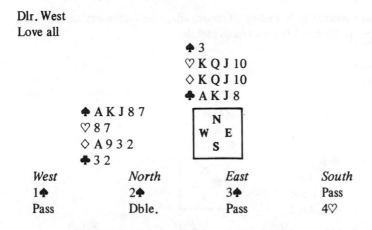

♠ 3
♥ K Q J 10
♦ K Q J 10
♣ A K J 8

♠ A K J 8 7
♥ 8 7
♦ A 9 3 2
♣ 3 2

West	North	East	South
1♠	2♠	3♠	Pass
Pass	Dble.	Pass	4♥

West leads the ♠K, East following with the ♠6 and declarer with the ♠2. What should West play next?

The natural play is a club, but it won't help. Either South will lose a club anyway, or he will have time to park a club on a diamond.

West must assume that East has the ♥A. That's pretty certain on the bidding, but even if it were otherwise, there can be no defence if he hasn't. The ♥A, then, will be the third trick. The best chance of a fourth is to find East with a doubleton diamond. West should, therefore, switch to the ♦2, leaving East with a diamond to return when he comes in with the ♥A.

♠ Q 6 5 4
♥ A 2
♦ 8 7
♣ 10 9 6 5 4

♠ 10 9 2
♥ 9 6 5 4 3
♦ 6 5 4
♣ Q 7

Couldn't East have a singleton diamond? Hardly. Knowing, when dummy goes down, that West needs the ♦A for his bid, he would have signalled loudly — with the ♠Q, no doubt — to alert him.

'Every picture tells a story.' The old adage holds the key to the right defence on this hand from a teams match.

Dlr. West
Love all

```
                        ♠ A 5 4
                        ♡ Q 9 8
                        ◇ A K 9 8
                        ♣ Q 6 5
        ♠ K 6               ┌─────────┐
        ♡ K 4 3             │    N    │
        ◇ 7 6 5 4           │  W   E  │
        ♣ K J 8 2           │    S    │
                            └─────────┘
```

West	North	East	South
Pass	1◇	1♠	2♡
Pass	2NT	Pass	3◇
Pass	3♡	Pass	4♡

West leads the ♠K to dummy's ♠A, East's card being the ♠J. The ♡Q comes next and West is in with the ♡K. How should he continue?

His first impulse will be to lead another spade, for didn't East signal loudly with the ♠J? After a moment's thought, West will see in that ♠J a warning. If East had the ♠Q, as well, that's the card he would have played. And if South has the ♠Q, another spade can be fatal.

The only hope of three quick tricks lies in clubs, and since East has nothing else, he surely has the ♣A. It may be a doubleton or he may have the ♣10 too. Either way, the ♣J is the right card to play, for the other hands may well be:

```
        ┌─────────┐       ♠ J 10 9 8 7 2
        │    N    │       ♡ 5 2
        │  W   E  │       ◇ J 10
        │    S    │       ♣ A 9 4
        └─────────┘
        ♠ Q 3
        ♡ A J 10 7 6
        ◇ Q 3 2
        ♣ 10 7 3
```

Suit Preference Signals lend themselves even more readily to abuse than most conventions. The idea is to use *unnecessarily* high or low cards to show interest in a higher or in a lower ranking suit. Unless, however, a signal is unmistakable, it will only confuse partner. Here is an example of a constructive signal from a minor tournament reported in the American *Bridge World*.

Dlr. South
Love all

```
                    ♠ 6 3 2
                    ♡ Q 3
                    ◇ K Q J 9 6 3
                    ♣ K 4
    ♠ A Q 8 7 5              ♠ 10 4
    ♡ 8 7 6          N       ♡ A 9 2
    ◇ A 4        W     E     ◇ 10 7 2
    ♣ 9 7 2          S       ♣ 10 8 6 5 3
                    ♠ K J 9
                    ♡ K J 10 5 4
                    ◇ 8 5
                    ♣ A Q J
```

South	West	North	East
1♡	1♠	2◇	Pass
2NT	Pass	3NT	

West leads the ♠7 to East's ♠10 and South's ♠J. The ◇K holds the next trick, East following with the ◇2. On the next diamond he plays the ◇10. West is in and must get a spade from East quickly. If East has an entry — if not, all is lost — where is it? This is where signals come in. East's ◇2 showed three diamonds, or he would have played high-low. Why, then, did he play the ◇10? Clearly it was a signal for a heart, the higher-ranking suit.

A useful gadget in defence, though little used in rubber bridge, is the trump signal. Here's an example:

Dlr. South
Love all

♠ J 7 2
♡ K Q 8
◇ Q 9 4
♣ K J 10 7

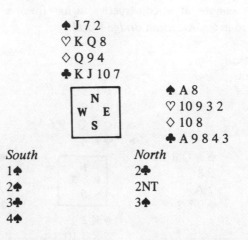

♠ A 8
♡ 10 9 3 2
◇ 10 8
♣ A 9 8 4 3

South	North
1♠	2♣
2♠	2NT
3♣	3♠
4♠	

West leads the ♣2. East wins and gives West a club ruff. Declarer wins the heart return and leads a spade. East rises with the ♠A and leads . . . another club? That will defeat the contract if West has a third trump. But South could have six spades, say:

♠ K Q 10 9 6 3 ♡ A 5 4 ◇ K ♣ Q 6 5.

Here, a third club is fatal. West can't ruff and the losing diamond disappears on dummy's fourth club.

A diamond return will be just as fatal, however, if South's hand is:

♠ K Q 10 9 5 ♡ A 4 ◇ A 3 2 ♣ Q 6 5.

Maybe one holding is more probable than the other, but East must guess — unless the partnership uses trump signals. Then, when a defender can ruff, he shows three trumps by playing high-low and only two by following in the natural, ascending order.

If West ruffed with the ♠4, then played the ♠3, East returns a club for West has a third trump. If, however, West ruffed with his lowest trump, he has no more and East leads a diamond.

Dlr. West
Both vul.

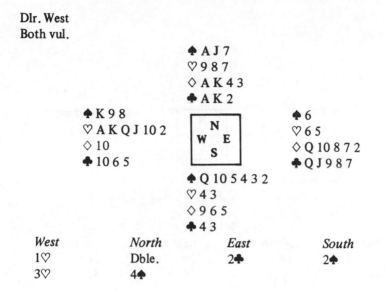

♠ A J 7
♥ 9 8 7
◇ A K 4 3
♣ A K 2

♠ K 9 8
♥ A K Q J 10 2
◇ 10
♣ 10 6 5

♠ 6
♥ 6 5
◇ Q 10 8 7 2
♣ Q J 9 8 7

♠ Q 10 5 4 3 2
♥ 4 3
◇ 9 6 5
♣ 4 3

West	North	East	South
1♥	Dble.	2♣	2♠
3♥	4♠		

It looks easy for South. The trump finesse being right, he will lose two hearts and a diamond. What else?

Ninety-nine Wests out of a hundred will lead out the three top hearts, East signalling with the ♣9 the third time.

The hundredth West will pause after the first two tricks to look for the other two needed to break the contract.

The diamonds may provide a trick, but the clubs can't, so a trump is the only hope.

If East has the ♠10 all is well, but even the ♠6 will suffice — if East uses it to ruff a heart, promoting a trick for West.

To make sure that East does his duty, West leads not a top heart but the lowly ♥2. The ♠6 forces out the ♠10 and now . . .

Did you back the defence? No? Quite right, for of course South doesn't have to over-ruff.

He discards a losing diamond, successfully negotiates the trump finesse and calls 'Table Up'.

Dlr. West
Love all

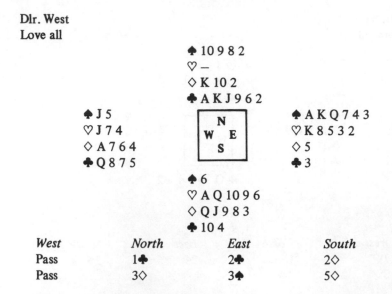

♠ 10 9 8 2
♡ —
◇ K 10 2
♣ A K J 9 6 2

♠ J 5
♡ J 7 4
◇ A 7 6 4
♣ Q 8 7 5

♠ A K Q 7 4 3
♡ K 8 5 3 2
◇ 5
♣ 3

♠ 6
♡ A Q 10 9 6
◇ Q J 9 8 3
♣ 10 4

West	North	East	South
Pass	1♣	2♣	2◇
Pass	3◇	3♠	5◇

East's 2♣ was conventional, asking for partner's better major. That's why South bid diamonds and not hearts.

West led the ♠J, overtaken by East who continued spades. South ruffed and led a trump.

The club finesse succeeds and West has no spade left with which to force declarer.

It looks good for South.

Sitting West, however, was world champion Jim Jacoby and when East produced a trump he could place every relevant card.

With a void in clubs, East wouldn't have overtaken the ♠J. Six spades, a diamond and a club left him with five (or four) hearts, so South had at least one heart loser, for he couldn't, on the bidding, have the ♡AKQ.

So Jacoby held up his ◇A until the third round and then played — the ♣Q!

That made good all dummy's clubs, but how could South draw the last trump? If he came back to his hand with the ♣10, he would be cut off from dummy. If he ruffed a spade, Jacoby would have trump control. Look out for variations on this theme. A defender's fourth trump can often be a thorn in declarer's side.

Dlr. South
Both vul.

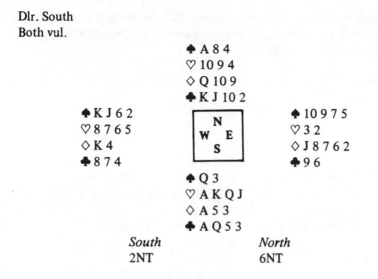

```
                         ♠ A 8 4
                         ♡ 10 9 4
                         ◇ Q 10 9
                         ♣ K J 10 2
      ♠ K J 6 2          ┌─────────┐          ♠ 10 9 7 5
      ♡ 8 7 6 5          │    N    │          ♡ 3 2
      ◇ K 4             │ W     E │          ◇ J 8 7 6 2
      ♣ 8 7 4           │    S    │          ♣ 9 6
                         └─────────┘
                         ♠ Q 3
                         ♡ A K Q J
                         ◇ A 5 3
                         ♣ A Q 5 3
```

South	*North*
2NT	6NT

West leads the ♡8. Shall we back declarer or defenders?

Declarer appears to have eleven tricks — four clubs, four hearts, two aces and the ◇Q, since West has the king. That leaves him one trick short.

South, however, is a resourceful player. He cashes his hearts and his clubs and plays the ◇A, then the ◇3. West is in and cannot avoid leading a spade away from his king to present declarer with his twelfth trick.

Did you back East-West? Quite right. West counts declarer's tricks, always the key to good defence. He cannot be sure that East has the ◇J — though it is the only honour he could have on the bidding — but he assumes that had declarer the ◇AJ, he would have taken the finesse. So West throws the ◇K under the ace. The ◇Q will take a trick, anyway, but only the eleventh. Now, however, West won't have to lead a spade and so present declarer with the twelfth. And when East comes in with the ◇J, he will lead a spade through South to beat the contract.

Winning Bridge

Bad bids sometimes meet with undeserved good fortune and then partner is quick to forgive, as so nearly happened on this deal in Hungary's
Individual Championship.

Dlr. West
E/W vul.

```
                         ♠9 5 3
                         ♡Q J 5
                         ◇9 7 4 2
                         ♣A Q 2
        ♠K Q 10 8 2                      ♠J 7 4
        ♡4              ┌─────────┐      ♡K 10 9 6 3 2
        ◇A J            │    N    │      ◇K Q
        ♣K 10 9 5 4     │ W     E │      ♣7 6
                        │    S    │
                        └─────────┘
                         ♠A 6
                         ♡A 8 7
                         ◇10 8 6 5 3
                         ♣J 8 3
```

West	North	East	South
1♣	Pass	1♡	1NT
Dble.	Pass	Pass	Pass

South's overcall was an abomination, but had East played better or
West not so well, the perpetrator would have scored a top.

West opened the ♠K and East, who should have dropped the ♠J,
played low. Fearing that declarer had ♠ A J 6, all set for the pro-
verbial Bath Coup, West switched to the ♡4.

The ♡Q, ♡K and ♡A made up the trick. A diamond followed.
Overtaking West's ◇J with his ◇Q East led the ♡10, clearing the suit.

What's the prognosis?

The kibitzers predicted an overtrick — until West smoothly jettisoned
his ◇A on East's ♡10!

Now East had an entry and South got his just deserts.

Observe that had East played his ♠J correctly at trick one, a spade
continuation would have presented South with his contract and injustice
would have triumphed once more.

Without the heart switch the defence would only come to four
spade tricks and two diamonds.

Now, had South won the first trick . . .

3   *Vanishing Tricks*

What happens when declarer has nine tricks and defenders have five? Does the immovable object give way to the irresistible force or does the force bow before the object?

The answer depends on the battle of communications as each side tries to keep open its own lines and to cut the enemy's. A winner is lost because the way to it is barred. Another, seemingly inaccessible, suddenly materialises through the creation of an unsuspected entry. Resource and ingenuity in killing and creating entries are features of the hands which follow. Before reading the analysis the reader may find it instructive to assess the chances of the two sides and, backing his judgment, forecast the result.

Dlr. South
Love all

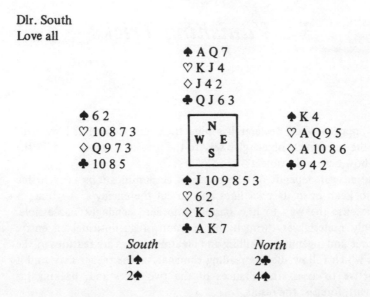

```
                 ♠ A Q 7
                 ♡ K J 4
                 ◇ J 4 2
                 ♣ Q J 6 3
♠ 6 2                           ♠ K 4
♡ 10 8 7 3          N          ♡ A Q 9 5
◇ Q 9 7 3       W     E        ◇ A 10 8 6
♣ 10 8 5            S          ♣ 9 4 2
                 ♠ J 10 9 8 5 3
                 ♡ 6 2
                 ◇ K 5
                 ♣ A K 7
```

South	North
1♠	2♣
2♠	4♠

West leads the ◇3. Which side will win? Have you placed your bets?

West wins the first trick with the ◇A and returns another diamond — or a club. It makes no difference. West is never on play again, so South clears trumps and discards a heart on dummy's fourth club. Contract made.

Did you back South?

We start again. East can see that unless West comes in to play a heart, the contract is undefeatable. There's no room for West to have the ♣K or the ♣A, but his opening lead suggests the ◇Q.

So, looking ahead at trick one, East plays the ◇10. South wins, but when East comes in with his ♠K he leads a diamond to West ◇Q and now a lethal heart pierces dummy's KJ4. One down.

Did you pick East-West?

Unlucky. At trick one, South goes up with dummy's ◇J, and now, no matter what East does, West can never gain the lead.

Many plays can be learned from textbooks. Many others must be found at the table and call for inspiration, as well as technique. This vintage hand is an example.

Dlr. South
Both vul.

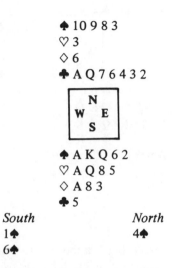

♠ 10 9 8 3
♡ 3
◇ 6
♣ A Q 7 6 4 3 2

♠ A K Q 6 2
♡ A Q 8 5
◇ A 8 3
♣ 5

South	North
1♠	4♠
6♠	

West leads the ◇K. South can see 12 tricks, if he can ruff four red losers in dummy. Communications, however, are uncertain. If he ruffs clubs twice to get back he may be over-ruffed and a trump return would spoil everything.

The club finesse suggests itself, but if it fails, declarer will have to find trumps 2-2 — or a bare ♠J — to set up the clubs and enjoy them.

When this hand came up, South found an ingenious solution. After the ◇A at trick one, he crossed to the ♣A, ruffed a club high and *led a low trump*. The ♠J took a trick to which it wasn't entitled, but declarer now had two entries to dummy, allowing him to set up the clubs and then get back to them.

♠ J 7 5
♡ K 9 6 2
◇ K Q 10 5
♣ J 8

♠ 4
♡ J 10 7 4
◇ J 9 7 4 2
♣ K 10 9

Dlr. West
N/S game

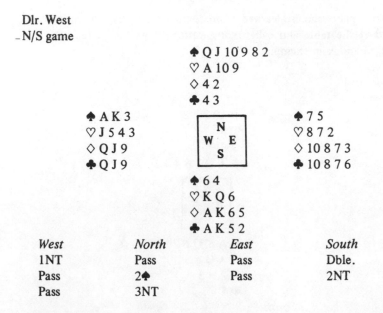

```
                      ♠ Q J 10 9 8 2
                      ♡ A 10 9
                      ◇ 4 2
                      ♣ 4 3
  ♠ A K 3                                  ♠ 7 5
  ♡ J 5 4 3              N                 ♡ 8 7 2
  ◇ Q J 9            W       E             ◇ 10 8 7 3
  ♣ Q J 9                S                 ♣ 10 8 7 6
                      ♠ 6 4
                      ♡ K Q 6
                      ◇ A K 6 5
                      ♣ A K 5 2
```

West	North	East	South
1NT	Pass	Pass	Dble.
Pass	2♠	Pass	2NT
Pass	3NT		

Pick the winner.

It's the wrong contract, but it's too late to worry about that now. West leads the ◇Q which is allowed to hold. He switches to the ♣Q and this, too, holds, East having encouraged in both minors. West persists with clubs.

Declarer wins and leads spades. West, of course, plays low the first time. Then, coming in with the ♠K, he leads his third club to South's ♣A.

What next?

Needing two entries to dummy, South cunningly underleads his ♡KQ and finesses. Luck is with him. The ♡10 holds and all is well — if West was asleep. Wide awake, however, West went up with the ♡J, killing dummy's second entry.

Did you back the defence? If so, you lose. Before touching hearts, South cashes his ◇AK, then he overtakes the ♡K with the ♡A and leads a spade to West's ace. West can only lead a heart, and wherever the ♡J may be, dummy's ♡10 is a certain entry.

Here's an easy looking contract from the National Pairs Championship of France. Only one pair made it, however, so any reader who fails will be in good company.

Dlr. South
Both vul.

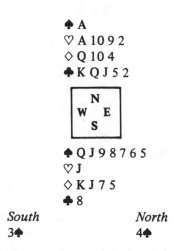

```
              ♠ A
              ♡ A 10 9 2
              ◇ Q 10 4
              ♣ K Q J 5 2
                   N
                 W   E
                   S
              ♠ Q J 9 8 7 6 5
              ♡ J
              ◇ K J 7 5
              ♣ 8
```

South	North
3♠	4♠

West leads the ◇8 to the ◇A. East returns the ◇2.

Declarer has a losing club and he has no remedy against a bad trump break. Can he make his contract if the trumps are divided reasonably?

The danger is obvious. West probably started with a doubleton diamond and East's return of the ◇2 looks like a suit preference signal, indicating the ♣A. So if West has ♠Kxx, he will put East in and get a diamond ruff. How can South prevent it?

The answer is to play the ♡A at trick three, then the ♡10, discarding the ♣8. If West goes up with an honour, South ruffs, crosses to the ♠A and leads the ♡9. Unless East has both the ♡K and ♡Q, declarer sheds his club and severs defenders' communications — the Scissors Coup.

```
♠ K 10 3                          ♠ 4 2
♡ K 7 6 4         N               ♡ Q 8 5 3
◇ 8 6          W     E            ◇ A 9 3 2
♣ 9 7 6 4         S               ♣ A 10 3
```

Dlr. West
Both vul.

```
              ♠ 5 4 3
              ♡ 8 7 3
              ◇ 7 5 3
              ♣ A K 10 3
```

```
              ♠ K Q J
              ♡ K Q 10 9 6 5
              ◇ K Q J
              ♣ 2
```

West	North	East	South
1♣	Pass	Pass	Dble.
Pass	1NT	Pass	4♡

West leads the ◇10 on which East plays the ◇9. How should declarer play?

It's obvious that East has the ◇A and is playing West for a doubleton. With three other losers – a trump, a diamond and a spade – South must avoid the threatened diamond ruff. He cannot avoid losing the lead, but he may be able to cut communications between East and West.

After winning the first diamond, he leads out dummy's ♣AK10 and – so long as East follows – he discards his ◇KQ. He loses a club instead of a diamond, but thereby averts the ruff.

```
♠ A 10 9 8                    ♠ 7 6 2
♡ A J            N             ♡ 4 2
◇ 10 2      W         E        ◇ A 9 8 6 4
♣ Q J 9 8 7      S            ♣ 6 5 4
```

South relies on losing only one trump. If West has ♡AJx, there's no hope. If East has ♡Jx, all is well and he can hardly have ♡Jxx, for with the bare ♡A, West wouldn't be looking for a ruff.

Dlr. West
Love all

```
                    ♠ Q 4
                    ♡ K 9 8 3 2
                    ◇ J 7 6
                    ♣ A 10 7
                    ┌─────────┐
                    │    N    │
                    │  W   E  │
                    │    S    │
                    └─────────┘
                    ♠ A J 10 9 6 5 3
                    ♡ –
                    ◇ K Q 10 5
                    ♣ 5 2
```

West	North	East	South
1♡	Pass	2♡	3♠
Pass	4♠		

West leads the ◇A and continues with the ♣4.

On the face of it, even if the trump finesse fails, declarer has only three losers — a trump, a diamond and a club.

West's opening lead of the ◇A, however, points to a singleton and the obvious danger is that should West come in with the ♠K, he will give East the lead with a club and ruff the diamond return.

South can improve his chances by giving up the trump finesse and laying down the ♠A. Now he will be safe unless West started with three trumps. What if he did? With a little forethought South can guard against this, too.

```
♠ K 8 2          ┌─────────┐          ♠ 7
♡ A J 6 5 4      │    N    │          ♡ Q 10 7
◇ A              │  W   E  │          ◇ 9 8 4 3 2
♣ J 8 6 4        │    S    │          ♣ K Q 9 3
                 └─────────┘
```

Going up with the ♣A at trick two, South leads dummy's ♡K. Unless East produces unexpectedly the ♡A, South discards his second club and remains in control. Whatever West returns, South wins and plays the ace and another trump.

'I could have saved a trick,' admitted the Professor, 'but it was worth an extra 100 for the chance of making the contract.'

'Was it in danger then?' asked the Senior Kibitzer innocently.

Dlr. South
Both vul.

```
                    ♠ 8 6 3
                    ♡ J 5
                    ◇ A J 10 9 8 5
                    ♣ 6 2
     ♠ K J 9 5          ┌─────┐          ♠ Q 7 2
     ♡ 10 8 6 4 2       │  N  │          ♡ Q 9 7
     ◇ 7 4             │W   E│          ◇ Q 6 2
     ♣ 9 4             │  S  │          ♣ K 10 8 7
                       └─────┘
                    ♠ A 10 4
                    ♡ A K 3
                    ◇ K 3
                    ♣ A Q J 5 3
```

South	*North*
2NT	3NT

West led the ♡4 to dummy's ♡J, East's ♡Q and South's ♡K.

Keeping the diamonds in reserve, the Professor began with the ♣A, then the ♣Q. Coming in with the ♣K, East returned a heart, knocking out the ♡A. The Professor now tried the diamonds, first the ◇K, then the finesse. Three down.

'What a distribution!' he exclaimed bitterly.

'A lucky one,' rejoined SK, 'but you failed to take advantage of it.

'At trick two you should have led the ◇3, finessing. If East wins, you have five diamond tricks, so he ducks and you take the club finesse. Next you overtake your ◇K and repeat the finesse. All that remains is to cash the ♣A and give up a club, scoring: four clubs, two diamonds, the ♡AK and the ♠A.

'You can't bring off a finesse, you know, if you don't take it,' observed SK philosophically. 'You had the two entries you needed and you lost them both,' he added unkindly.

Dlr. West
E/W vul.

　　　　　　　　♠ J 9 8 7
　　　　　　　　♡ 5 4
　　　　　　　　◇ A 4
　　　　　　　　♣ K 10 7 4 3

```
        N
    W       E
        S
```

　　　　　　　　♠ Q 10 5 4
　　　　　　　　♡ A K 9
　　　　　　　　◇ 3 2
　　　　　　　　♣ A J 6 5

West	North	East	South
1♡	Pass	Pass	Dble.
Pass	2♣	Pass	2♠
Pass	3♣	Pass	3NT
Pass	4♠		

North might have bid 1♠ rather than 2♣ in response to South's double. Relying on the club fit, however, South chanced his arm, so luckily the spade fit came to light after all.

West led the ♣8. How should South play?

The ♣8 is clearly a singleton and it is very likely, on the bidding, that West has both tops in trumps. If so, he will have time to drive out the ◇A and then to put East in with a diamond to get his club ruff.

What can declarer do about it?

The answer is to win the first trick with the ♣K and lead a heart, inserting the ♡9. If West switches to a diamond, South goes up with the ◇A and cashes the ♡AK, discarding dummy's ◇4. Having exchanged one loser for another, so severing communications between defenders, South can now attend to the trumps.

　　♠ A K 6　　　　　　　　　♠ 3 2
　　♡ Q J 10 8 3　　```   ```　♡ 7 6 2
　　◇ Q J 10 9　　　 W   E　　◇ K 8 7 6 5
　　♣ 8　　　　　　　　S　　　　♣ Q 9 2

Dlr. West
Both vul.

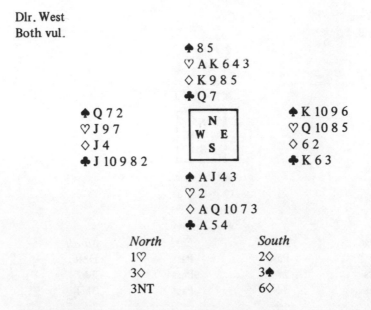

♠ 8 5
♡ A K 6 4 3
◇ K 9 8 5
♣ Q 7

♠ Q 7 2
♡ J 9 7
◇ J 4
♣ J 10 9 8 2

♠ K 10 9 6
♡ Q 10 8 5
◇ 6 2
♣ K 6 3

♠ A J 4 3
♡ 2
◇ A Q 10 7 3
♣ A 5 4

North	*South*
1♡	2◇
3◇	3♠
3NT	6◇

West leads the ♣J. East covers dummy's ♣Q and declarer's prospects look bleak. Surely South was too ambitious.

Assuming a favourable distribution, as declarer must always do when no other will help, how should he play?

The hearts must be 4-3 and the trumps 2-2. Then dummy's hearts will take care of declarer's two losing clubs and two spades can be ruffed in dummy. A spade will be the only loser.

If you go through the motions, however, you will find that declarer will be short of an entry in dummy, for he must ruff two hearts and then get back to the table without losing the lead.

So, after the ♣A, he leads a heart to the ♡A and ruffs a low heart with *an honour*. Then he plays a trump, finessing the ◇9. If West rises with the ◇J, the ◇K goes up, but South still has a diamond lower than dummy's 9 and, therefore, the additional entry he needs. Had he ruffed the first heart low, that entry would not be available.

I was kibitzing a high-powered game at the St James's Bridge Club, where Britain's leading players get together.

Dlr. North
Love all

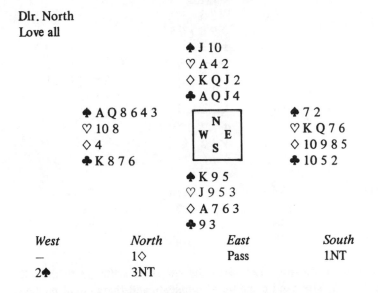

	♠ J 10	
	♡ A 4 2	
	◇ K Q J 2	
	♣ A Q J 4	
♠ A Q 8 6 4 3		♠ 7 2
♡ 10 8	N	♡ K Q 7 6
◇ 4	W E	◇ 10 9 8 5
♣ K 8 7 6	S	♣ 10 5 2
	♠ K 9 5	
	♡ J 9 5 3	
	◇ A 7 6 3	
	♣ 9 3	

West	North	East	South
—	1◇	Pass	1NT
2♠	3NT		

West led the ♣6, dummy's ♣10 winning. Declarer continued with the ◇K, then the ◇Q. Had the suit broken 3-2, it would have yielded two entries to the closed hand, the ◇A3. The 4-1 split proved fatal, for with one entry only the club finesse couldn't be repeated and two club tricks weren't enough.

The pretty idea of using the ◇3 as an entry didn't impress unduly a fellow kibitzer. 'Why,' he asked, 'didn't declarer overtake dummy's ♠10 with his K? How could this lose? If the club finesse fails, the ♠K is useless as-a stopper, anyway.

'If it succeeds, it isn't needed — except as an entry.'

Dlr. East
Game all

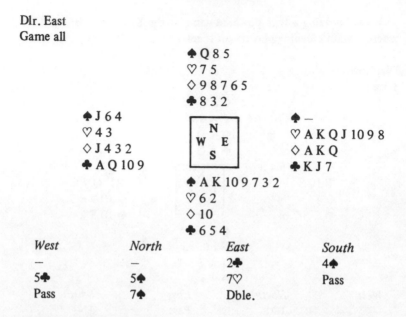

♠ Q 8 5
♡ 7 5
◇ 9 8 7 6 5
♣ 8 3 2

♠ J 6 4
♡ 4 3
◇ J 4 3 2
♣ A Q 10 9

♠ —
♡ A K Q J 10 9 8
◇ A K Q
♣ K J 7

♠ A K 10 9 7 3 2
♡ 6 2
◇ 10
♣ 6 5 4

West	North	East	South
—	—	2♣	4♠
5♣	5♠	7♡	Pass
Pass	7♠	Dble.	

After winning the first trick with the ♡K, East switched to the ◇K, then the ◇A. The hand came up at duplicate and there could be a big difference between going down six or only five. Against East-Wests who stopped in 6♡, scoring 1460 — all would doubtless make thirteen tricks — 1400 would show a profit, while 1700 wouldn't. How, then, should South have played?

What happened was that he ruffed with the ♠7, and though he cursed himself in the same breath, it was too late to take it back.

Dummy's diamonds alone could yield an extra trick and it needed three entries to set one up and then enjoy it. East's 7♡ bid showed that he couldn't have a spade, so South led the ♠2 and finessed the ♠5 confidently. After ruffing a diamond high, he played the ♠3, hoping to win with dummy's ♠8. West, however, jumped up with the ♠J, driving out the ♠Q, and South had no spade lower than the ♠8. If only he had cursed himself a split second earlier and retained the ♠7!

Dlr. South
Love all

```
                    ♠ K
                    ♡ K Q J 5 3
                    ◇ K 3 2
                    ♣ 10 8 7 6
              ┌───────────┐
              │     N     │
              │  W     E  │
              │     S     │
              └───────────┘
                    ♠ A Q 2
                    ♡ 8 7
                    ◇ A 7 6 4
                    ♣ A 9 4 3
```

South	North
1♣	1♡
1NT	3NT

West leads the ♣J. How should South play?

This calls for a standard safety play and can be worked out at the table, if declarer recognises the situation in time.

If the hearts split 3-3 there's no problem, so declarer must guard against the more probable 4-2 break. Should he lead a top heart at trick two, the defender with the ace will hold off.

Now, with one entry only in dummy, declarer won't be able to set up the hearts and get back to enjoy them.

When this hand came up, South was America's Harold Ogust. At trick two he led a low heart and the defence was helpless.

```
   ♠ J 10 9 8 4      ┌───────────┐     ♠ 7 6 5 3
   ♡ 4 2             │     N     │     ♡ A 10 9 6
   ◇ Q 5             │  W     E  │     ◇ J 10 9 8
   ♣ K J 5 2         │     S     │     ♣ Q
                     └───────────┘
```

East made the best return, the ◇J, but Ogust won in his hand and had a heart to play, driving out the ♡A. The ◇K remained as an entry to three good hearts in dummy.

Dlr. East
Both vul.

```
                    ♠ Q J 10 7 4
                    ♡ 6 4 3 2
                    ◇ J
                    ♣ Q 9 5
```

```
                    ♠ A K
                    ♡ A K Q J 5
                    ◇ Q 4
                    ♣ A 8 4 2
```

West	North	East	South
−	−	1◇	Dble.
2◇	2♠	4◇	4♡
Pass	Pass	5◇	Pass
Pass	5♡		

West led the ◇2 to East's ◇K. ◇A followed. There was nothing diabolical about the distribution and no way in which defenders could beat
5♡ − on their own. Nevertheless, declarer went down. Where did he
go wrong?

The 'natural' play is to ruff the second diamond and draw trumps.
If they break 3-1, however, declarer will need a lot of luck with the
clubs.

No luck will be needed however, as long as East is allowed to hold
his ◇A at trick two. Should he lead a third diamond, South would ruff
high in his hand, draw trumps, taking three rounds, if need be, and cash
the ♠AK. He would then overtake his ♡5 with dummy's six and enjoy
the spades.

```
    ♠ 9 8 6 3 2                    ♠ 5
    ♡ 7                            ♡ 10 9 8
    ◇ 9 8 5 2                      ◇ A K 10 7 6 3
    ♣ 7 6 3                        ♣ K J 10
```

To preserve the ♡6 as an entry, declarer cannot afford to ruff the
◇A in dummy.

Dlr. South
Love all

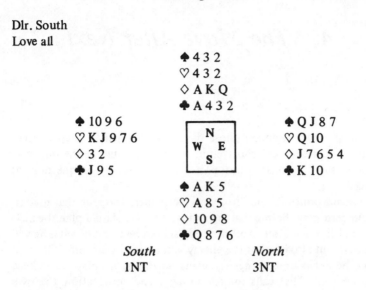

```
              ♠ 4 3 2
              ♡ 4 3 2
              ◇ A K Q
              ♣ A 4 3 2
♠ 1 0 9 6                        ♠ Q J 8 7
♡ K J 9 7 6       N             ♡ Q 10
◇ 3 2         W       E          ◇ J 7 6 5 4
♣ J 9 5           S             ♣ K 10
              ♠ A K 5
              ♡ A 8 5
              ◇ 10 9 8
              ♣ Q 8 7 6
```

South	North
1NT	3NT

Which side shall we back? West leads the ♡7 to East's ♡Q and the suit is continued, declarer holding up his ♡A twice. This is the moment for bets.

South leads dummy's ♣A and ♣2. East is in, but he has no more hearts, so declarer is home.

East, however, can do better. He knows that West cannot have an ace and that his only possible entry must be in clubs, so on the third heart he jettisons his ♣K. Now South can only make two clubs before letting West in.

Give South another chance. He wins the second heart, crosses to the ◇A and leads a low club. If East goes up with the ♣K it's all over, so he plays the ♣10. South's ♣Q wins and he leads another club, West playing the ♣J. If East started with a doubleton ♣K, as above, South must duck. If East has the missing ♣9, South must play the ♣A and a third club. It's a guess. Bets are off, the result being a draw.

4 *The Move After Next*

Even comparative beginners these days have learned to prepare their opening bids. Hence the short club, allowing a rebid at the one level over any suit response from partner. It is simply a question of looking ahead.

The same principle and the same mechanics, too, for that matter, apply in card play. Before making a move a player should plan the next one — and the one after. And not only should he think of what he will do himself, but also of what the enemy will do to thwart him. With that in mind he draws up contingency plans, so timing his plays as to keep a step in front. That calls for forethought and anticipation, the twin motif of the hands which follow.

It's always tantalising to have tricks and no apparent way of getting at them. That was the problem facing Omar Sharif on this hand during a match in Italy.

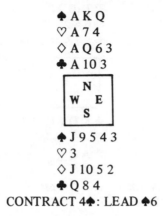

♠ A K Q
♡ A 7 4
◇ A Q 6 3
♣ A 10 3

♠ J 9 5 4 3
♡ 3
◇ J 10 5 2
♣ Q 8 4

CONTRACT 4♠: LEAD ♣6

On the second round of trumps, West discarded the ♡9. Can Omar make the contract?

Ten tricks are there — five trumps, three diamonds and two aces. The snag is that declarer can only get to his hand to draw trumps by ruffing a heart, and if he does that, he will have no trump left to stop the hearts which opponents will surely unleash if the ◇K is wrong.

Omar Sharif found a neat solution. After cashing dummy's three top spades, he led a low heart. No matter what opponents did next, Omar was in control. With the ♡A still in dummy, he could afford to ruff a heart, leave himself without a trump, and set up his diamonds.

The East-West hands were:

♠ 6
♡ K 10 9 6 5
◇ 9 7 4
♣ K 9 5 2

♠ 10 8 7 2
♡ Q J 8 2
◇ K 8
♣ J 7 6

Dlr. West
Both vul.

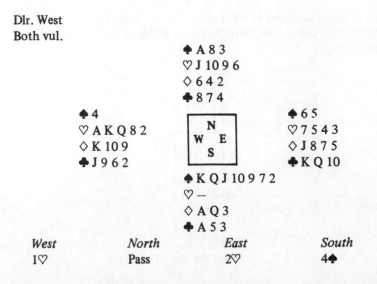

♠ A 8 3
♥ J 10 9 6
♦ 6 4 2
♣ 8 7 4

♠ 4
♥ A K Q 8 2
♦ K 10 9
♣ J 9 6 2

♠ 6 5
♥ 7 5 4 3
♦ J 8 7 5
♣ K Q 10

♠ K Q J 10 9 7 2
♥ —
♦ A Q 3
♣ A 5 3

West	*North*	*East*	*South*
1♡	Pass	2♡	4♠

West leads the ♡K. Given the 2-1 trump break, can declarer ensure his contract against any distribution that the evil spirits can conjure up? If so, how should he set about it?

In view of West's bid, South doesn't expect the diamond finesse to succeed, so he can see four losers, two in clubs and two in diamonds.

Fortunately he can find two more in hearts, should he need them, and by exchanging losers he can turn one of them into a winner.

A moment's carelessness, however, may lose the contract before it can be won. South must ruff the ♡K high, for the seven and two of spades have a vital role to play.

At trick two, declarer overtakes his ♠K with dummy's ♠A and leads the ♡J, throwing a club.

West switches to a club knocking out the ♣A, but South is a move ahead. He overtakes his ♠7 with the ♠8 and leads the ♡10, discarding his last club.

The ♡9 is now a trick, declarer's tenth, and the ♠3 is an entry, for South still has the ♠2.

Two kibitzers, waiting to cut in, sat behind South.

Dlr. West
Love all

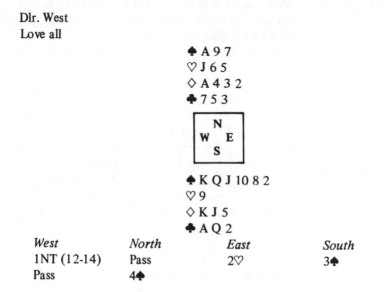

```
              ♠ A 9 7
              ♡ J 6 5
              ◇ A 4 3 2
              ♣ 7 5 3

              ♠ K Q J 10 8 2
              ♡ 9
              ◇ K J 5
              ♣ A Q 2
```

West	North	East	South
1NT (12-14)	Pass	2♡	3♠
Pass	4♠		

West led out the king and ace of hearts. South ruffed and continued with the ♠K, then the ♠10 to dummy's ♠A, both defenders following.

'We shan't be in after this hand,' said the first kibitzer, shaking his head. 'On the bidding, every missing honour must be wrong.'

'Precisely,' rejoined the second kibitzer, 'but since declarer knows it, just as we do, he can make the contract.'

As he spoke, South led dummy's ♡J, covered with the ♡Q by East and ruffed in the closed hand. Now came the key play – the ♣2. East overtook West's six with the nine and returned the ◇8. South, however, was a move ahead. Playing in the knowledge that East would never be in again, he won in dummy – and cashed the ♣A. Then he exited with the ♣Q.

```
♠ 6 5                        ♠ 4 3
♡ A K 10                     ♡ Q 8 7 4 3 2
◇ Q 10 9 7                   ◇ 8 6
♣ K J 6 4                    ♣ 10 9 8
```

West was forced to lead a diamond or the thirteenth club, presenting South with a ruff and discard.

One of the simplest ways of making tricks is by means of a cross-ruff. Declarer must remember to cash his tricks in the side-suits, in case one of them is ruffed when opponents end up with all the trumps, but the rest is easy — when the hand lends itself to it.

Often, however, the cross-ruff must be carefully timed, as here:

```
                    ♠ Q J 10
                    ♡ 7 6 3
                    ◇ Q J
                    ♣ Q 8 6 5 3
    ♠ 9 7 6 5 3          ┌─────────┐          ♠ 4
    ♡ A K 9 5            │    N    │          ♡ Q J 8 4 2
    ◇ 8 6               │ W     E │          ◇ 10 9 7 4
    ♣ 10 7              │    S    │          ♣ K J 9
                        └─────────┘
                    ♠ A K 8 2
                    ♡ 10
                    ◇ A K 5 3 2
                    ♣ A 4 2
```

CONTRACT 4♠: LEAD ♡K

South ruffs the heart continuation and embarks on a cross-ruff. What should be his sequence of plays?

In the event, he cashed the ◇QJ, came to hand with the ♣A and led the ◇A, ruffed by West and over-ruffed in dummy. Returning with a heart ruff, South led his ◇K, once more ruffed and over-ruffed. Now, alas, South couldn't get back to his hand to play another diamond without giving up the lead to East, who promptly returned a trump, killing the tenth trick.

To make his contract, South must *overtake* dummy's second diamond to lead another. This gives him the extra entry to score three tricks by ruffing diamonds in dummy.

Dlr. North
Love all

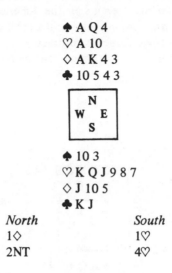

♠ A Q 4
♥ A 10
♦ A K 4 3
♣ 10 5 4 3

♠ 10 3
♥ K Q J 9 8 7
♦ J 10 5
♣ K J

North	South
1♦	1♥
2NT	4♥

At first sight, South should bid 3NT rather than 4♥, since it is easier to make nine tricks than ten. But with something to spare, South can afford the premium of an extra trick to ensure against what might happen in spades.

West leads the ♦7. How should South play?

The temptation is to play low from dummy. If East wins and switches to a club, and there are two club losers, declarer still has ten tricks.

The danger is that the ♦7 could be a singleton and South cannot afford to have a diamond ruffed. A spade switch might then be disastrous. To avoid the risk, he should go up with the ♦A, draw trumps and concede two clubs.

♠ J 9 8 7
♥ 6 5 3 2
♦ 7
♣ A Q 9 8

♠ K 6 5 2
♥ 4
♦ Q 9 8 6 2
♣ 7 6 2

Even if West comes in twice, he cannot lead both a spade and a second diamond (if he had one) before South has time to set up dummy's ♣10 for his tenth trick.

The diagrammed hand came up in the semi-finals of the Vanderbilt Cup, one of the two main events in the American bridge calendar. Declarer, a world champion, missed a brilliant play which would have brought home an otherwise hopeless contract.

Even with all four hands on view, the reader will be doing well to spot it.

Dlr. North
N/S vul.

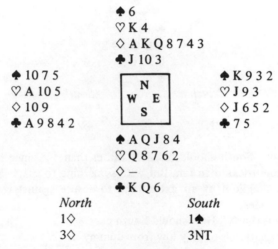

```
                        ♠ 6
                        ♡ K 4
                        ◊ A K Q 8 7 4 3
                        ♣ J 10 3
        ♠ 10 7 5                              ♠ K 9 3 2
        ♡ A 10 5           N                  ♡ J 9 3
        ◊ 10 9          W     E               ◊ J 6 5 2
        ♣ A 9 8 4 2        S                  ♣ 7 5
                        ♠ A Q J 8 4
                        ♡ Q 8 7 6 2
                        ◊ —
                        ♣ K Q 6
```

	North		*South*
	1◊		1♠
	3◊		3NT

West opened the ♣4. Winning with the ♣10 in dummy, declarer led out the top diamonds. When West showed out, he had to give up the suit, for the defence would have had time to set up their clubs before he could get back to enjoy the diamonds. The result was one down.

Where did South go wrong?

In the vital race between clubs and diamonds, declarer could have won the day — had he jettisoned his ♣KQ on dummy's diamonds. Now he can safely lead a fourth diamond, for defenders cannot clear clubs without giving dummy an entry with the ♣J. And if they keep off clubs, South can reach dummy via the ♡K.

Dlr. South
N/S vul.

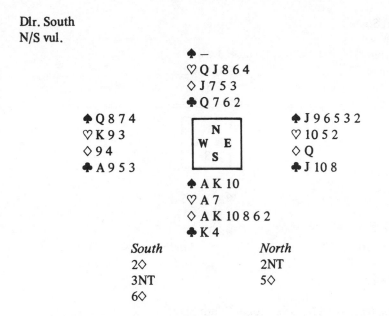

```
              ♠ —
              ♡ Q J 8 6 4
              ◇ J 7 5 3
              ♣ Q 7 6 2
♠ Q 8 7 4                          ♠ J 9 6 5 3 2
♡ K 9 3          N                ♡ 10 5 2
◇ 9 4        W       E            ◇ Q
♣ A 9 5 3        S                ♣ J 10 8
              ♠ A K 10
              ♡ A 7
              ◇ A K 10 8 6 2
              ♣ K 4
```

South	North
2◇	2NT
3NT	5◇
6◇	

The bidding is a matter of style, but the final contract is eminently reasonable. If the ♡K is on the right side, there's no problem. The question is: can the contract be made if the ♡K is wrong?

Declarer, when this hand came up, was Fanny Parienté, one of France's leading players. Winning the opening trump lead with the ◇A, she immediately played the ♣4. Had West gone up with the ♣A, she would have cashed the ♣K and discarded her ♡7 on dummy's ♣Q. But West, of course, played low, allowing the ♣Q to win.

Fanny Parienté came back to her hand with a trump, cashed the ♠AK, throwing two clubs from dummy, ruffed the ♠10 and exited with a club, throwing West in with the ♣A.

What could he do but play away from his ♡K or present declarer with a ruff and discard?

The timing of the hand is all-important. To preserve communications, declarer cannot afford to play a second round of trumps before leading the ♣4.

Dlr. South
E/W vul.

♠ J 7 4
♡ Q 7 3 2
◇ 7 5
♣ A Q J 9

```
    N
  W   E
    S
```

♠ A 6
♡ A K 9 5 4
◇ K 6 4 2
♣ 10 3

South	West	North	East
1♡	1♠	3♡	Pass
4♡			

West leads the ♠K. How should South play?

On his vulnerable overcall, West probably has the ◇A. If he has the ♣K, too, there's no problem, but the danger is that East will come in with it to lead a diamond through the closed hand.

How, then, can declarer avoid losing a spade, a club and two diamonds? The answer is to draw trumps — they are 3-1 — and lead a spade. Winning with the ♠Q, West will, no doubt, switch to a club. South will go up with the ♣A, discard a club on the ♠J and take a ruffing finesse in clubs. If East has the ♣K, there will be no club loser. If he hasn't, South will discard a diamond. Whether or not West leads his ◇A, it will be his last trick, for dummy's clubs will take care of two more of South's diamonds. The lucky spade lead allows declarer to keep one step ahead of the defence.

♠ K Q 10 9 5 2
♡ 8
◇ A Q 3
♣ 7 6 2

```
    N
  W   E
    S
```

♠ 8 3
♡ J 10 6
◇ J 10 9 8
♣ K 8 5 4

'It isn't only that I hold bad cards,' explained East to his Guardian Angel, 'even when I do get anything, every finesse is wrong. Now why doesn't it happen to other people?'

The GA waved his magic wand.

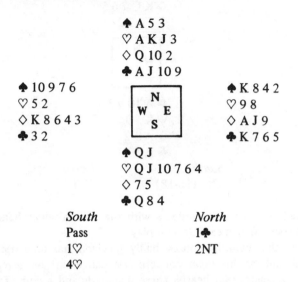

    ♠ A 5 3
    ♡ A K J 3
    ◇ Q 10 2
    ♣ A J 10 9

♠ 10 9 7 6   ♠ K 8 4 2
♡ 5 2   ♡ 9 8
◇ K 8 6 4 3   ◇ A J 9
♣ 3 2   ♣ K 7 6 5

    ♠ Q J
    ♡ Q J 10 7 6 4
    ◇ 7 5
    ♣ Q 8 4

South	North
Pass	1♣
1♡	2NT
4♡	

West led the ◇4 and East's ◇J captured dummy's ◇10. The ◇A and ◇9 followed, but a chord had snapped already on the GA's harp. What had gone amiss?

Three finesses out of three were wrong for South, and West's lead hadn't helped, yet he made his contract with six trumps, three clubs and the ♠A.

As he thought back· on the play, the scales fell from East's eyes. If South had a third diamond, it couldn't escape. A spade could – and did.

At trick two, East should have returned the ◇9, not the ◇A, allowing West to lead a spade through dummy before South could come in to draw trumps and clear clubs.

Dlr. South
N/S vul.

```
              ♠ J 4
              ♡ Q 10
              ◇ K Q 7 6 5
              ♣ J 4 3 2
```

```
              ┌─────────┐
              │    N    │
              │  W   E  │
              │    S    │
              └─────────┘
```

```
              ♠ A 10 9 3
              ♡ K J 9
              ◇ A 3 2
              ♣ A 10 9
```

South	*North*
1NT (16-18)	3NT

West leads the ♡3. East follows with the ♡4. In which hand do you win the trick? Which card do you play next?

Unless the diamonds break badly, declarer has nine tricks. That, then, should be his main concern. He can count on seven certain tricks — a spade, two hearts, three diamonds and a club. The spades are unlikely to provide two more tricks, so he must look to the clubs. If the honours are split or if East has both, the clubs may make up for the diamonds. But there's no time to lose.

The first trick is won in dummy and a finesse in clubs is lost to West, who continues hearts.

```
   ♠ K 8 7 6                         ♠ Q 5 2
   ♡ A 7 6 3 2      ┌─────────┐      ♡ 8 5 4
   ◇ 4              │    N    │      ◇ J 10 9 8
   ♣ Q 8 7          │  W   E  │      ♣ K 6 5
                    │    S    │
                    └─────────┘
```

Declarer is a move ahead. He leads the ◇A and ◇2. If, as above, the diamonds are 4-1, he takes a second finesse in clubs, cashes the ♣A and crossing to the ◇Q, scores dummy's long club for his ninth trick.

Dlr. North
Love all

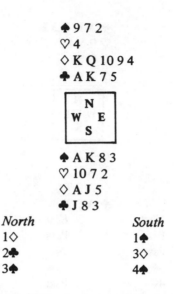

♠ 9 7 2
♡ 4
◇ K Q 10 9 4
♣ A K 7 5

♠ A K 8 3
♡ 10 7 2
◇ A J 5
♣ J 8 3

North	South
1◇	1♠
2♣	3◇
3♠	4♠

South knows that North has only three spades, but he knows also that the hearts are wide open. With more than enough for game and no hope in notrumps, he has little choice. To pass 3♠ would surely be craven.

West leads the ♡Q and switches to the ♣10. How should South play?

Usually, with a 4-3 trump fit, declarer ducks on the first round so as to retain control in the event of the probable 4-2 break. The danger here is that the defence would set up a club before the diamonds could be run.

Declarer does best to go up with the ♣A, cross to the ♠A and ruff a heart. Coming back with the ◇J, he ruffs another heart, takes the ◇A and cashes the ♣K. Now comes a third diamond. Let either defender ruff.

♠ Q J 6 4
♡ Q J 9 8 6
◇ 7 3
♣ 10 4

♠ 10 5
♡ A K 5 3
◇ 8 6 2
♣ Q 9 6 2

With two trumps to West's one (after the ruff), South has time to discard his club loser on a diamond.

Dlr. West
N/S vul.

```
                        ♠ A K Q 3 2
                        ♡ 9 5 4 2
                        ◇ Q 8
                        ♣ Q 4
      ♠ J 7 5                                    ♠ 10 9 8 6
      ♡ Q J 10          ┌─────────┐              ♡ 2
      ◇ K J 10 3 2      │    N    │              ◇ 5 4
      ♣ K J             │  W   E  │              ♣ 10 9 8 7 6 5
                        │    S    │
                        └─────────┘
                        ♠ 4
                        ♡ A K 8 7 6
                        ◇ A 9 7 6
                        ♣ A 3 2
```

West	North	East	South
1NT	Pass	Pass	Dble.
Pass	Pass	2♣	2♡
Pass	3♣	Pass	3◇
Pass	4♡	Pass	6♡

The North-South bidding is courageous, but knowing, on West's open-ing, that the hand can be played double dummy, the urge to stretch is understandable.

West leads the ♡Q. Declarer wins and takes his second top heart. Will he make his contract?

Yes, declarer should get home, yet he can easily go wrong. After the ♡AK, he plays the ♠AK, discarding a diamond. Next a spade is ruffed and West is thrown in with a trump. It is immaterial from which king he decides to lead. South goes up with dummy's queen and throws two losers from the other minor on the ♠Q2.

Suppose, however, that declarer cashes the ♠Q before ruffing a spade. It looks innocuous, yet the contract is now doomed. West returns the suit from which South discarded on the ♠Q and a loser in the other minor at once springs to life.

5   Crystal Gazing

By counting the cards as they fall, pip by pip and suit by suit, the experienced player soon sees in his crystal a vivid picture of opponents' cards. But, as any clairvoyant will confirm, the crystal is sometimes clouded. Then to peer through the mist calls for what are known as 'discovery plays'. Locating the ace in one suit helps to find the king in another, for given the bidding, the same player can't have both. When the division of the cards in two suits is known, testing a third will pinpoint the distribution in the fourth.

Reading opponents' cards brings rich rewards. No less rewarding is skill in reading their minds. And just as every bid and every pass tells a story, so does the play of every card — or the failure to play it. Why doesn't declarer in 3NT develop his long suit? Can it be that he is trying to steal his ninth trick? Why won't East give West a second ruff? Doesn't he expect him to have another trump? As he gazes into his crystal, the reader will find inferences in plenty, positive and negative, to dispel the thickest mist.

'One day,' said the Professor bitterly, 'I'll find a king on the right side of an ace.'

'You found one just now,' rejoined the Senior Kibitzer. 'It didn't help you very much.'

Dlr. East
Love all

```
                      ♠ Q 2
                      ♡ J 4 3
                      ◇ 8 7 3 2
                      ♣ Q J 10 9
      ♠ K 10 9 6                        ♠ 5 4 3
      ♡ Q 10 5 2          N             ♡ A K 9 8 7 6
      ◇ K J 10 9      W       E         ◇ Q 4
      ♣ 4                 S             ♣ 3 2
                      ♠ A J 8 7
                      ♡ —
                      ◇ A 6 5
                      ♣ A K 7 6 5 4
```

West	North	East	South
–	–	Pass	1♣
Pass	2♣	2♡	3♡
4♡	Pass	Pass	5♣

West led the ♡2 to East's ♡K. The Professor had bid somewhat optimistically, yet all he needed was the spade finesse. So he took it without further ado. When the ♠J lost to West's ♠K, the Professor conceded defeat.

'Didn't you know that West had the ♠K?' asked S.K. rhetorically. 'On that bidding, you couldn't suspect him of underleading his ♡A. So East was marked with six hearts to the AK. And he had to have the ◇Q or ◇J, too, for holding the ◇KQJ, West would have led the ◇K rather than the ♡2.

'How, then, could East, who passed as dealer, have the ♠K, as well? Clearly,' went on SK remorselessly, 'you should have played a low spade towards dummy, losing a trick to the ♠K and later discarding two losing diamonds on the ♠AJ.'

Dlr. East
N/S vul.

```
              ♠ A 7 2
              ♡ A 9 8 6 5
              ◊ 10
              ♣ Q 10 8 3
                                   ♠ 6
              ┌──────────┐         ♡ —
              │    N     │         ◊ 8 7 6 3 2
              │  W   E   │         ♣ K J 9 7 6 5 4
              │    S     │
              └──────────┘
```

West	North	East	South
—	—	3♣	4♠
Pass	6♠		

West led the ♡K. Declarer played low from dummy and East looked intently through the backs of the cards. What did he see and how did he set out to beat the contract?

Ready? Then let us follow East's gaze. He would see no club in West's hand, for with the A, A2 or singleton 2, he would have doubtless led the suit. How many hearts did he have? With eight to a hundred honours he would surely have sacrificed in 5♡ at favourable vulnerability. But he must have seven since with two hearts South couldn't afford to duck. With one only he was right to play low, avoiding the risk of a ruff and retaining the ♡A till later — an ideal parking place for the ♣2.

Having seen enough, East ruffed his partner's ♡K and returned a club for West to ruff. The other hands were — they simply had to be:

```
      ♠ J 3
      ♡ K Q 10 7 4 3 2     ┌──────────┐
      ◊ Q J 9 5            │    N     │
      ♣ —                  │  W   E   │
                           │    S     │
                           └──────────┘
              ♠ K Q 10 9 8 5 4
              ♡ J
              ◊ A K 4
              ♣ A 2
```

Dlr. West
Love all — N/S 30

```
                          ♠ J 10 9
                          ♡ A J 6 5
                          ◇ K J 6
                          ♣ 10 6 3
                       ┌─────────┐
                       │    N    │
                       │  W   E  │
                       │    S    │
                       └─────────┘
                          ♠ A K Q
                          ♡ Q 10 9 8 7
                          ◇ 4 2
                          ♣ J 4 2
```

West	North	East	South
1NT (12-14)	Pass	Pass	2♡
Pass	3♡		

West led out the ♣AKQ and switched to the ◇5. Which card should South play from dummy? As declarer pondered, two Junior Kibitzers exchanged views.

'Just about an even money chance,' said the first JK.

'Not quite,' rejoined the second. 'West's 1NT leaves precious little for East. The ◇K is the card to play.'

'On the contrary,' declared the Senior Kibitzer, who had overheard the juniors. 'South has no choice. He must play the ◇J.

'Having lost three clubs,' went on SK, 'he cannot afford to lose a trump. So he plays West for the ♡K. That's the key to the diamonds, for it gives West 12 points in clubs and hearts. He cannot have the ◇A for his 12-14 notrump. South must play for the only distribution, consistent with the bidding, to give him his contract, which is:

```
     ♠ 8 4 3 2                          ♠ 7 6 5
     ♡ K 4           ┌─────────┐        ♡ 3 2
     ◇ Q 7 5 3       │    N    │        ◇ A 10 9 8
     ♣ A K Q         │  W   E  │        ♣ 9 8 7 5
                     │    S    │
                     └─────────┘
```

♠ A K Q J 7 6      ♠ 10 4
♡ 2   ♡ J 9 8 7
◇ A J 3   ◇ K 9 8 2
♣ 7 6 5   ♣ A K 4

CONTRACT 6♠: LEAD: ♡K

The bidding isn't impeccable and is best forgotten. Suffice it to say that over West's opening 1♠, North called 2♡.

After ♡K, North led the ♡A. Declarer ruffed, crossed to the ♠10 and took the vital finesse in diamonds. When the ◇J held, he began to see daylight. If all went well, dummy's last diamond would take care of the losing club.

Two more rounds of trumps followed, North showing up with three, South with a doubleton. Next came the ◇A, bringing the ◇Q from South. Was the ◇10 lurking behind it? That was the question and the contract hinged on finding the right answer. Where should West look for it?

No guess is involved. Declarer goes over to the ♣A, cashes the ♣K — North discarding a heart — and ruffs a heart. If South shows out, North must have six hearts. He followed to one club and to three spades, ten cards in all. So he cannot have four diamonds and the ◇10 must drop. Had South found another heart, North would be marked with four diamonds.

'The odds against this distribution . . .' began the Professor.
'True,' agreed the Senior Kibitzer, 'but what was wrong with it?'

Dlr. South
Love all

♠ 4 3 2
♡ Q 9 7
◇ K 7 4 2
♣ Q 10 9

♠ A K Q J 7
♡ –
◇ Q J 6
♣ A J 8 7 5

South	North
1♣	1◇
2♠	2NT
3♠	4♠
6♠	

West led the ♡J. The Professor ruffed, drew trumps in three rounds and
led the ◇Q, then the ◇J, West playing high-low, the ◇9 before the ◇3.
East rose with the ◇A and returned the ♡K, driving out declarer's last
trump. The Professor crossed to the ◇K, all following, and took the
club finesse. Three down.

♠ 10 9 8   N   ♠ 6 5
♡ J 10 8 6 3 2 W   E   ♡ A K 5 4
◇ 10 9 3   S   ◇ A 8 5
♣ K   ♣ 6 4 3 2

'Why do you suppose that West followed high-low in diamonds?' asked
SK severely. 'He produced a third diamond and he couldn't have four.
Why, then, the false signal? Clearly because he didn't want East to hold
up his ◇A. Again, why? Because he badly wanted you to have an entry
in dummy to take the club finesse and that could only be important
to him if he had the ♣K — bare. East set a trap and you promptly
fell into it. 'Not such a hostile distribution, after all, was it?'

Dlr. South
Love all

$$\spadesuit \text{ A K 8 7}$$
$$\heartsuit \text{ Q}$$
$$\diamondsuit \text{ 5 4}$$
$$\clubsuit \text{ K 9 8 7 6 5}$$

```
      N
  W       E
      S
```

$$\spadesuit \text{ J 6 3}$$
$$\heartsuit \text{ 3 2}$$
$$\diamondsuit \text{ A Q J 10 9 8}$$
$$\clubsuit \text{ A J}$$

South	West	North	East
1◇	Pass	2♣	2♡
3◇	Pass	3♠	Pass
4♣	Pass	4♡	Pass
6◇			

West leads the ♡J.

Winning with the ♡K, East switches to the ♠9, covered by South's ♠J, West's ♠Q and dummy's ♠K. The trump finesse follows and the ◇Q holds. How should declarer continue?

South's first thought is to repeat the trump finesse. Should he, then, lead a spade, inserting dummy's ♠8, or should he cross to the ♣K?

Neither course is satisfactory, because East's ♠9, though it may be a singleton, needn't be a true card, and if it isn't, South will have to set up the clubs to take care of a spade and a heart. For the same reason, he cannot use the ♣K as an entry prematurely.

The solution is to lead the ◇A, fully expecting to drop East's ◇K. Why? Because if East had a third diamond he would have killed the contract stone dead at trick two by leading his ♡A and forcing dummy.

$$\spadesuit \text{ Q 5 4 2}$$
$$\heartsuit \text{ J 10 9}$$
$$\diamondsuit \text{ 7 6 3}$$
$$\clubsuit \text{ Q 10 2}$$

```
      N
  W       E
      S
```

$$\spadesuit \text{ 10 9}$$
$$\heartsuit \text{ A K 8 7 6 5 4}$$
$$\diamondsuit \text{ K 2}$$
$$\clubsuit \text{ 4 3}$$

The odds against picking up thirteen cards of a suit can only be expressed in terms of light years, but it keeps on happening for all that, usually on 1 April. Very occasionally, it occurs in a goulash, when, after a throw-in, the cards are not shuffled and are dealt three and four at a time, sometimes in two sets of five, then three.

Goulashes are rarely played in Britain, but they enjoy a certain popularity in Paris. Here is one featured in *Le Bridgeur*.

Dlr. East
Both vul.

	♠ A J		♠ K 9 7 6 5 2
	♡ –	N	♡ –
	◊ A Q J 8 5 4	W E	◊ K 10 7 3
	♣ A 9 5 3 2	S	♣ K J 8

West	North	East	South
–	–	1♠	7♡
7NT			

The immediate jump to 7♡ isn't very subtle, and holding three aces, West can easily deduce that South must have all thirteen hearts. Against that West has no defence and any penalty will show a big profit. So he is only too willing to sacrifice. But when dummy goes down, the question arises: with every card marked by South's revealing bid, need it be a sacrifice?

North leads a diamond. Winning in his hand, declarer finesses the ♣8. Back in his hand with a diamond, he finesses the ♣J and cashes the ♣K. Another diamond takes him back to the closed hand, and after cashing the ♣A, he reels off the rest of the diamonds. North must find a discard from ♠Q108 ♣Q. He is helpless.

West's thirteenth trick will be either his ♣9 or dummy's ♠9.

Two-plus-one needn't always make three, not if declarer looks carefully through the backs of the cards. Here is an example from the Belgian National Championships.

Dlr. East
Love all

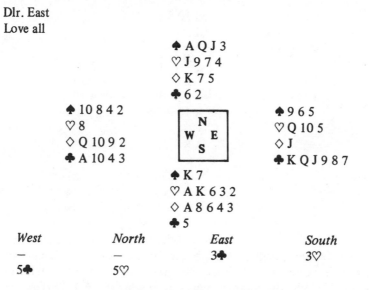

West	North	East	South
—	—	3♣	3♡
5♣	5♡		

West led the ♣A and a second club, ruffed by South. The contract appears to depend on not losing a trump, and when West showed out, the kibitzers shook their heads. And yet declarer made his contract. No luck or guesswork came into it.

South simply counted East's cards. He was marked on his bid with at least six clubs and he was known to have three hearts, leaving four cards in spades and diamonds. So South cashed the ◇K and led a diamond to his ace. Had East followed, South would have played spades until East ruffed. If he didn't he would have been thrown in with the ♡Q. Either way, he would have had to concede a ruff and discard. As it was, it wouldn't have helped East to ruff a loser, so he shed a spade. He was thrown in with a trump just the same — after the spades had been cashed, of course.

Dlr. West
N/S vul.

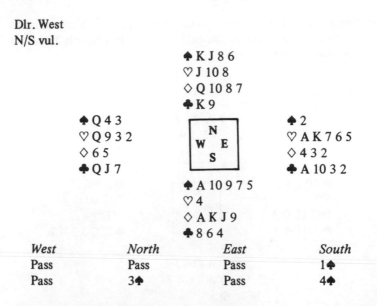

	♠ K J 8 6		
	♡ J 10 8		
	◇ Q 10 8 7		
	♣ K 9		

♠ Q 4 3   ♠ 2
♡ Q 9 3 2   ♡ A K 7 6 5
◇ 6 5   ◇ 4 3 2
♣ Q J 7   ♣ A 10 3 2

♠ A 10 9 7 5
♡ 4
◇ A K J 9
♣ 8 6 4

West	North	East	South
Pass	Pass	Pass	1♠
Pass	3♠	Pass	4♠

West leads the ♡2. East wins with the ♡K and continues with the ♡A.

While declarer ponders, two kibitzers have a look at East's hand and make a bet. One backs declarer, the other takes defenders. With the ♣A over the ♣K, the contract hinges on finding the ♠Q. Declarer can play for the drop or he can finesse either way, so the first kibitzer lays 7-4 on him. Was the second kibitzer wise to accept these odds?

Mathematicians needn't bother to work out percentages. Declarer can hardly go wrong. Without so much as a glance in his crystal, he should lay down the ♠A and finesse against West. What's more, it needn't worry him unduly if the finesse fails.

The key to the play, as so often happens, lies in the bidding. East, who passed, has shown up with the ♡AK. If he has the ♠Q, he can hardly have the ♣A as well. And if he has the ♣A, he isn't likely to have the ♠Q. Either way, the contract should be safe.

Technique has many facets. Not the least important is forethought. An example is this hand played by Des Deery of Northern Ireland in a match against Scotland.

Dlr. East
Love all

```
                    ♠ K
                    ♡ 6 5 2
                    ◊ A 9 7 5
                    ♣ A K Q 7 4
        ♠ 10 9 6 5        N         ♠ A Q 7 3 2
        ♡ Q 9 3       W       E     ♡ A 10 8 4
        ◊ J 6             S         ◊ 4 3 2
        ♣ J 9 6 3                   ♣ 5
                    ♠ J 8 4
                    ♡ K J 7
                    ◊ K Q 10 8
                    ♣ 10 8 2
```

West	North	East	South
—	—	1♠	Pass
1NT	Dble.	2♡	2NT
Pass	3NT		

West led the ♠5 to East's ♠A. Going up with the ♠J on the spade continuation, Deery had to find eight more tricks without losing the lead. How should he play?

At trick three, Deery led the ♣8, the key card. After the ♣A came three rounds of diamonds, ending in the closed hand, then the ♣10. West played low — and Deery ran it!

He could count East for nine cards in the majors and he had shown three diamonds, so his ♣5 had to be a singleton.

Had West covered the ♣10, Deery would have later finessed against the ♣9. The ♣8 would have blocked the suit, but now all was well.

Picking the winner after the race saves a lot of guesswork, as on this hand from a teams match.

♠ K 4 3
♡ A K 2
◇ A 8 7
♣ A 6 5 2

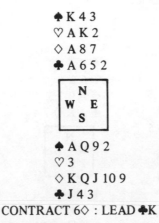

♠ A Q 9 2
♡ 3
◇ K Q J 10 9
♣ J 4 3

CONTRACT 6◇ : LEAD ♣K

Declarer sees eleven tricks and can make another, either by setting up a long club, if the clubs break 3-3, or by bringing in four spades.

Clubs come first. South goes up with the ♣A, plays the ♡AK, discarding a club, and then a second club. East shows out, so all hinges on the spades.

Ruffing West's club return, South draws trumps — West follows three times — and ruffs dummy's third heart. West follows.

Now only spades remain. Declarer leads the ♠A and ♠2 to dummy's ♠K. West's cards are the ♠5 and ♠10, and East's the ♠6 and ♠7. Should declarer play for the drop or insert the ♠9 when East plays the ♠8 on the third round?

No guess is involved. West has shown five clubs, three hearts and three diamonds. He cannot have a third spade. The finesse is a certainty.

♠ 10 5   ♠ J 8 7 6
♡ J 8 7   ♡ Q 10 9 6 5 4
◇ 4 3 2   ◇ 6 5
♣ K Q 10 9 8   ♣ 7

When both sides bid, declarer can often pick up clues about the distribution. It requires more skill to draw inferences from opponents' passes in an uncontested auction, as here.

Dlr. South
N/S vul.

```
            ♠ A K 6 2
            ♡ K Q 3
            ◇ J 6 2
            ♣ 7 4 2
        ┌─────────┐
        │    N    │
        │ W     E │
        │    S    │
        └─────────┘
            ♠ Q 4
            ♡ 6 4 2
            ◇ K Q 10 9 3
            ♣ A K 6
```

South	West	North	East
1◇	Pass	1♠	Pass
1NT	Pass	3NT	

West led the ♡J. Reasoning that if West had the ♡A and he ducked in the dummy, he would look remarkably foolish, declarer went up with the ♡K — and lived to regret it.

West's pass was the key to the right play. Since, at favourable vulnerability, he couldn't bid 1♡ over 1◇, he could hardly have ♡AJ1098 and also the ◇A, and without the ◇A he would have no entry, so it would be safe to play low from dummy at trick one. The other hands were:

```
♠ 10 8 3           ┌─────────┐        ♠ J 9 7 5
♡ J 10 9 8 5       │    N    │        ♡ A 7
◇ A 4              │ W     E │        ◇ 8 7 5
♣ 10 5 2           │    S    │        ♣ Q J 9 8
                   └─────────┘
```

Couldn't East have a third heart? Certainly, but then West would have only four and could hurt no one. And if East had a doubleton ♡A, as above, ducking in dummy would block the suit and the contract would be safe.

Dlr. West
Love all

          ♠ 9 2
          ♡ J 3
          ◇ A K J 7
          ♣ Q 8 6 5 4

```
        N
    W       E
        S
```

          ♠ Q 10 8 7 6 5
          ♡ A K 9 7
          ◇ 3
          ♣ 10 7

West	*North*	*East*	*South*
Pass	1◇	Pass	1♠
Pass	2♣	Pass	2♡
Pass	2♠	Pass	3♠

West leads the ♣K and ♣A, East following in ascending order, and then switches to a low heart. Dummy's ♡J holds. How should declarer play?

Declarer has no loser in the side suits, but having lost two tricks already, he cannot afford to lose more than two trumps. The natural play is to run dummy's ♠9, hoping to find East with the ♠J. This time, however, the situation calls for the 'unnatural'.

Once again the key to the play is in the bidding. West, who passed as dealer, has already produced the ♣AK and he must surely have the ♡Q, too, for otherwise East would have covered dummy's ♡J. So West is unlikely to have another king, let alone an ace, though he may well have a knave.

Having built up this picture, South leads the ♠9, and if East plays low, goes boldly up with his ♠Q.

   ♠ J 3
   ♡ Q 8 6 5 4
   ◇ 10 4 2
   ♣ A K 9

```
        N
    W       E
        S
```

   ♠ A K 4
   ♡ 10 2
   ◇ Q 9 8 6 5
   ♣ J 3 2

'Double dummy, I could have made it,' sighed the Professor.
'And that's how you should have played it,' said the Senior Kibitzer.

Dlr. West
Love all

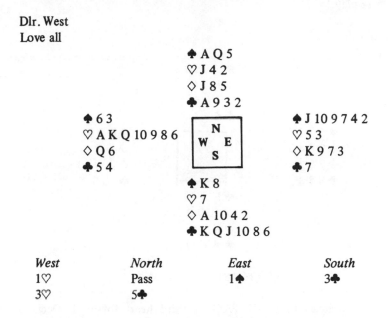

	♠ A Q 5	
	♡ J 4 2	
	◇ J 8 5	
	♣ A 9 3 2	

♠ 6 3   ♠ J 10 9 7 4 2
♡ A K Q 10 9 8 6   ♡ 5 3
◇ Q 6   ◇ K 9 7 3
♣ 5 4   ♣ 7

♠ K 8
♡ 7
◇ A 10 4 2
♣ K Q J 10 8 6

West	*North*	*East*	*South*
1♡	Pass	1♠	3♣
3♡	5♣		

West led the ♡K, then the ♡A. The Professor ruffed, drew trumps, ruffed dummy's last heart and cashed the ♠AKQ. All now hinged on not losing two diamonds.

The Professor led dummy's ◇5 and inserted the ◇10, losing to West's ◇Q. Another diamond came back but with the K9 poised over the knave, defeat was unavoidable.

'You had a complete count on West's hand,' said SK severely. 'He had shown up with seven hearts and two black doubletons, so he was marked with two diamonds.

'After the spades, you run the ◇J. If West wins, he must lead another diamond up to your ◇A10 or give you a ruff and discard. Should East cover the ◇J, you win, cross to dummy and again lead a diamond. It doesn't matter if West wins for he has no more diamonds and must, willy-nilly, present you with your eleventh trick.'

I am indebted to Albert Dormer, for many years the Editor of the International Bridge Press Association's *Bulletin*, for this sad story of a clever play.

Dlr. South
Both vul.

```
                    ♠ A J 10 6
                    ♡ K J 6
                    ◇ J 8 4
                    ♣ 9 7 4
   ♠ 5 3 2                         ♠ Q 9 7
   ♡ 9 8 4 3          N            ♡ A Q 5
   ◇ 7 5 2         W     E         ◇ A Q 10 3
   ♣ 8 5 3            S            ♣ 10 6 2
                    ♠ K 8 4
                    ♡ 10 7 2
                    ◇ K 9 6
                    ♣ A K Q J
```

South	North
1NT (16-18)	3NT

West led a heart to East's ♡AQ. A third heart followed. Declarer crossed to his ♣K and finessed the ♠J.

East knew exactly what an unkind fate had in store for him. On his opening bid, South was marked with every missing honour card. So he would score three spades, a heart and four clubs, and, needing one more trick, he would lead a diamond from dummy and make his ◇K.

To thwart an unkind fate, East found a brilliant stratagen. When South inserted dummy's ♠J, East ducked nonchalantly. Not knowing who had the ◇A, South would naturally repeat the spade finesse. Now East would pounce and exit with a club, cutting declarer off for evermore from dummy.

Alas, when East played low to the ♠J, West stretched out his hand to collect the trick. South gave East a dirty look and laid down the ♠A. So fate won after all.

6   *Legerdemain*

The counterpart to reading opponents' cards is to make them misread ours. Many stratagems in this area have become standardised. Inhibitory bids, false signals, pseudo-singletons, camouflage and concealment in every form weave the everyday pattern of deception. And yet there's always room for the unexpected, opportunities to hoodwink, to surprise, to set traps for the unwary. As the reader is about to see, ingenuity and improvisation are the salient features in the mechanics of deception.

Many players derive more pleasure from a good swindle than from the most brilliant coup. So says H.W. Kelsey in a study of advanced hocus-pocus. Here's an example.

Dlr. North
N/S vul.

```
              ♠ 7
              ♡ A K J 10 5
              ◇ A K
              ♣ Q 8 6 5 2
♠ Q 10 6 4 3              ♠ K 9 5 2
♡ 9 8 7        N         ♡ Q 6 2
◇ J 9 7 6 2   W   E      ◇ 10 5 4
♣ —             S        ♣ K J 3
              ♠ A J 8
              ♡ 4 3
              ◇ Q 8 3
              ♣ A 10 9 7 4
```

North	South
1♡	2♣
4♣	4♠
5NT	6♣

North's 5NT is 'Josephine' asking partner to bid the grand slam if he has two of the three top honours in clubs.

West leads the ♡9 and, sitting East, you have a premonition of disaster. If declarer knows his business, he can't fail to make his contract. At trick two he will lead dummy's ♣2 and cover your ♣3. Any low card will do. It's a standard safety play to ensure the loss of one trump trick only.

What can you do about it? Technically nothing, but a little imagination may take the place of a lot of technique.

On dummy's ♡K try dropping your ♡Q – without a trace of hesitation of course. Having no reason to doubt that it's a singleton, declarer won't dare to take the safety play. He will surely lead a trump to his ace and that will be that.

West led the ♣2. 'Do you make us 70 up?' asked South. East agreed.

Some players, especially when stakes are high, keep a running total of the score. This tells them how many tricks are needed to affect the rubber points.

At 70 up, making ten or eleven tricks wouldn't help. Unless South could make twelve, he might as well settle for nine.

This gave East an idea.

```
                    ♠ A Q J 3
                    ♡ 9 5
                    ◇ K Q 3
                    ♣ Q 10 9 8
       ♠ 5 4                          ♠ 10 8 7 6
       ♡ A Q J 8 6 4    ┌─────────┐   ♡ 10 7
       ◇ 8              │    N    │    ◇ 10 9 5 4 2
       ♣ 7 6 5 2       │  W   E  │    ♣ K J
                       │    S    │
                        └─────────┘
                    ♠ K 9 2
                    ♡ K 3 2
                    ◇ A J 7 6
                    ♣ A 4 3
```

South	West	North	East
1◇	1♡	1♠	Pass
1NT	Pass	3NT	

Can you see what was in East's mind?

West's heart-holding could be deduced from his passive lead. Meanwhile declarer could clearly count on spades and diamonds for eight tricks. The ♣A would be his ninth, unless . . .

On dummy's ♣8 East smoothly went up with the ♣K! Now South saw a happy mirage. By taking and repeating the 'marked' finesse against the ♣J, he could make twelve tricks.

Disdaining to cash his four diamonds first, he took the club finesse without further ado.

East pounced and promptly shot his ♡10 through the closed hand.

The mirage vanished. Of South's twelve tricks only six remained.

The mere mention of Italy evokes the image of the legendary Blue Team. But more than thirty years ago, before the Squadra Azzura was born, the Italians were already making headlines.

One of their most colourful players was Mario Franco, inventor of the Marmic system, the most bizarre ever to be played in first-class bridge up to that time.

Franco was as ingenious in dummy play as in bidding. This was one of his exploits.

Dlr. South
N/S vul.

```
                    ♠ 10 7 3 2
                    ♡ J 4 3 2
                    ◇ 8 5 4
                    ♣ 8 6
   ♠ Q J 8 6                          ♠ A 9 4
   ♡ Q 10 8 6 5         N             ♡ A K 9 7
   ◇ J 9 3 2        W       E         ◇ Q 10 6
   ♣ —                  S             ♣ 9 5 4
                    ♠ K 5
                    ♡ —
                    ◇ A K 7
                    ♣ A K Q J 10 7 3 2
```

South	West	North	East
2♣	3♣	Pass	Pass
6♣	Pass	Pass	Dble.

No one seemed to take West's intervention seriously. The point of the hand, however, is in the play.

West led the ♠Q to East's ♠A. How did Mario Franco bring home the impossible contract?

On the ♠A Franco calmly dropped the ♠K! Ruffing the ♡A which came next, he reeled off his trumps. Both defenders, of course, 'knew' what to keep. Declarer could be counted for eight trumps, the bare ♠K and no hearts. Therefore he must have four diamonds. So West kept ◇J932 and East the ◇Q106, and dummy's ♠107 scored the last two tricks.

The hand below, described by José le Dentu in *Le Figaro*, is a pretty exercise in legerdemain.

Dlr. West
Love all

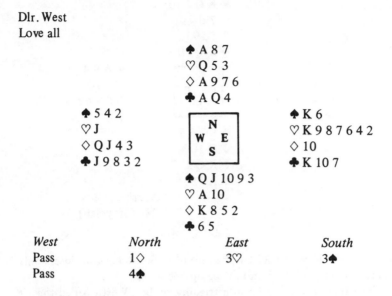

♠ A 8 7			
♡ Q 5 3			
◇ A 9 7 6			
♣ A Q 4			

♠ 5 4 2   ♠ K 6
♡ J   ♡ K 9 8 7 6 4 2
◇ Q J 4 3   ◇ 10
♣ J 9 8 3 2   ♣ K 10 7

♠ Q J 10 9 3
♡ A 10
◇ K 8 5 2
♣ 6 5

West	North	East	South
Pass	1◇	3♡	3♠
Pass	4♠		

West led the ♡J. Declarer, who appears to have a losing spade, a losing club and at least one losing diamond, is in imminent danger of a heart ruff. And yet he made his unmakable contract!

From the first, the ♡J looked every inch a singleton, so, to avoid a ruff, if the spade finesse failed, South tried to create the illusion that he was the one with the singleton heart.

Instead of covering the ♡J to promote a 'certain' trick, he played low from dummy and winning with the ♡A, took the losing trump finesse. The ◇10 came back. South took the trick in his hand, cleared trumps, ending in dummy, and led a low heart. East had no thought of letting South ruff his ♡K and make dummy's ♡Q good, so he played low. What East wouldn't?

Declarer's ♡10 won and it was all over. His only losers were a spade, a diamond and a club. Two others had disappeared.

Dlr. South
E/W vul.

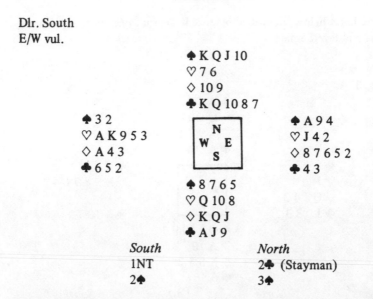

```
                    ♠ K Q J 10
                    ♡ 7 6
                    ◇ 10 9
                    ♣ K Q 10 8 7
  ♠ 3 2                              ♠ A 9 4
  ♡ A K 9 5 3          N             ♡ J 4 2
  ◇ A 4 3          W       E         ◇ 8 7 6 5 2
  ♣ 6 5 2              S             ♣ 4 3
                    ♠ 8 7 6 5
                    ♡ Q 10 8
                    ◇ K Q J
                    ♣ A J 9
```

South	*North*
1NT	2♣ (Stayman)
2♠	3♠

Which side shall we back? On the face of it, South has four losers only. Can the defence induce him to develop one more?

When this hand came up in a friendly rubber, West opened the ♡K and East looked everywhere for a fifth trick. He could count two hearts, his ♠A and an outside trick with which partner was marked on the bidding.

The defence had one other asset, East's ♠9. Somehow it had to be made to yield a trick. So, on the ♡K East signalled loudly with the ♡J, echoing with the ♡2 on the ♡A. West continued with the ♡9 — showing interest in diamonds as opposed to clubs — and declarer, fearing a ruff, played one of dummy's trump honours. When East followed, the scales fell from South's eyes, but it was too late. Coming in with the ♠A, East put his partner in with the ◇A and another heart assured a second trump trick for the defence.

Necessity is not only the mother of invention, but of deception, too, sometimes, as on this hand in the Swedish Pairs Championship.

Dlr. South
N/S vul.

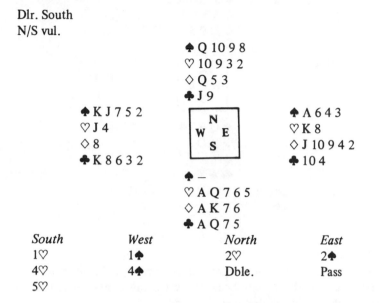

♠ Q 10 9 8
♡ 10 9 3 2
◇ Q 5 3
♣ J 9

♠ K J 7 5 2
♡ J 4
◇ 8
♣ K 8 6 3 2

♠ A 6 4 3
♡ K 8
◇ J 10 9 4 2
♣ 10 4

♠ —
♡ A Q 7 6 5
◇ A K 7 6
♣ A Q 7 5

South	West	North	East
1♡	1♠	2♡	2♠
4♡	4♠	Dble.	Pass
5♡			

What can be the problem? Surely every South in the room will make twelve tricks, losing only one club. And yet, without doing anything unreasonable, one declarer went down.

Ruffing the spade lead, he crossed to the ◇Q and took the losing club finesse. The club return was won in dummy and now it was time for the trump finesse. Nothing wrong so far.

On declarer's ♡Q, however, West smoothly dropped the ♡J. It could cost him nothing, for the defence had no legitimate claims to another trick. But the false trail set South on the road to ruin. Other declarers would pick up the ♡K and make twelve tricks, so he had to do likewise. Needing, as he thought, another entry in dummy to repeat the trump finesse, he ruffed a club. East promptly over-ruffed and returned a diamond, whereupon West suddenly discovered the ♡4.

Dlr. South
Love all

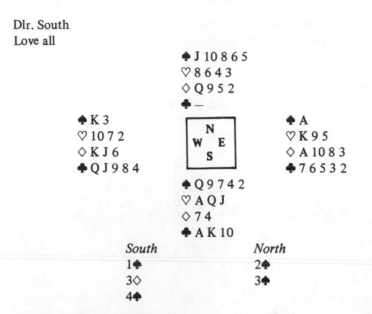

```
                        ♠ J 10 8 6 5
                        ♡ 8 6 4 3
                        ◇ Q 9 5 2
                        ♣ —
      ♠ K 3                                    ♠ A
      ♡ 10 7 2            ┌─────────┐          ♡ K 9 5
      ◇ K J 6             │    N    │          ◇ A 10 8 3
      ♣ Q J 9 8 4         │ W     E │          ♣ 7 6 5 3 2
                          │    S    │
                          └─────────┘
                        ♠ Q 9 7 4 2
                        ♡ A Q J
                        ◇ 7 4
                        ♣ A K 10
```

South	North
1♠	2♣
3◇	3♠
4♠	

South's 3◇ was a diversion intended to inhibit a diamond lead. It succeeded admirably, if only because West didn't contemplate leading the suit in the first place. He opened the ♣Q.

Assuming perfect defence, what is the likely outcome? Even with the ♡K on the right side, declarer has four inescapable losers. Can one of them, by virtue of some Houdini act, contrive to escape?

When this hand occurred, declarer found an ingenious solution. He set up dummy's long heart! It doesn't seem to add up, but there is, in fact, no possible defence.

Ruffing the ♣Q in dummy, declarer takes the heart finesse. Next, he ruffs his ♣K and finesses again. Then he cashes the ♡A, bringing down the ♡K and crosses to dummy by ruffing his ♣A. It only remains to shed a diamond on the thirteenth heart, not caring who does what.

No declarer in the finals of the French National Pairs championship succeeded in making 4♡ here:

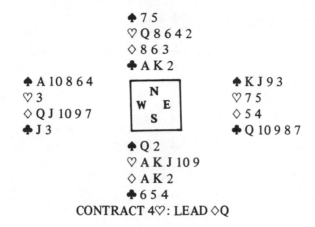

```
                    ♠ 7 5
                    ♡ Q 8 6 4 2
                    ◇ 8 6 3
                    ♣ A K 2
    ♠ A 10 8 6 4        N          ♠ K J 9 3
    ♡ 3              W     E       ♡ 7 5
    ◇ Q J 10 9 7        S          ◇ 5 4
    ♣ J 3                          ♣ Q 10 9 8 7
                    ♠ Q 2
                    ♡ A K J 10 9
                    ◇ A K 2
                    ♣ 6 5 4
```

CONTRACT 4♡: LEAD ◇Q

Every South ended up by conceding four seemingly inevitable losers — two spades and a trick in each minor. And yet one of those losers can be made to vanish into thin air.

South wins the first trick, draws trumps and leads a spade. The defence, let us say, persist with diamonds. Declarer wins, cashes the ♣AK and exits with his second spade. Either defender can win. If it's West, he can cash a diamond, but having no more clubs, he must concede a ruff and discard. The club loser disappears.

If East wins the second spade, he can cash a club. Now the ensuing ruff and discard takes care of the losing diamond.

Of course, if defenders switch to clubs after winning the first spade, declarer cashes the ◇K, as well as his second top club, before exiting with a spade.

The key to the play is to visualise each defender, in turn, with a doubleton in one of the minors.

Many a contract can only be made with the help of East or West and not the least of declarer's arts lies in knowing how to propitiate them.

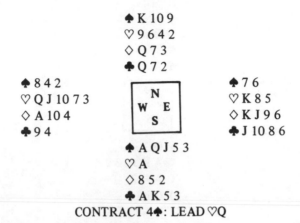

                ♠ K 10 9
                ♡ 9 6 4 2
                ◇ Q 7 3
                ♣ Q 7 2

♠ 8 4 2   ♠ 7 6
♡ Q J 10 7 3   ♡ K 8 5
◇ A 10 4   ◇ K J 9 6
♣ 9 4   ♣ J 10 8 6

                ♠ A Q J 5 3
                ♡ A
                ◇ 8 5 2
                ♣ A K 5 3

CONTRACT 4♠: LEAD ♡Q

South quickly counted nine tricks — five spades, the ace of hearts and three top clubs. A 3-3 club break would yield the tenth trick. Could he do better?

Yes. If the suit broke 4-2, after two rounds of trumps, the defender with the doubleton club might not have the last trump. The French call this the *'manoeuvre de Guillemard'*, and it improves declarer's chances.

But South might do better still. If he could ruff three hearts in his own hand, he would have ten tricks — dummy's three trumps, the ace of hearts, the three heart ruffs and the ace, king, queen of clubs.

Unfortunately, dummy is an entry short for a dummy reversal.

When this hand was played, South found a subtle solution. At trick two, he led a diamond. There was no future in the suit, but it gave East — who won the trick — the chance to return a heart, which was just as good as an extra entry in dummy.

Dlr. South
Love all

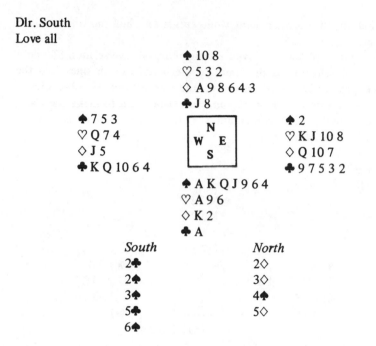

♠ 10 8
♥ 5 3 2
♦ A 9 8 6 4 3
♣ J 8

♠ 7 5 3
♥ Q 7 4
♦ J 5
♣ K Q 10 6 4

♠ 2
♥ K J 10 8
♦ Q 10 7
♣ 9 7 5 3 2

♠ A K Q J 9 6 4
♥ A 9 6
♦ K 2
♣ A

South	North
2♣	2♦
2♠	3♦
3♠	4♠
5♣	5♦
6♠	

Shall we back South to make 6♠ or defenders to defeat him? Ready?
Rien ne va plus.

West leads the ♣K. Declarer must bring in the diamonds and rightly
fears a 3-1 trump break. So, at trick two, he leads the ♦K, the ♦2 to
the ♦A and another diamond which he ruffs low. Deliberately, he
courts an over-ruff, for once West parts with a trump — unless it's a
singleton — he can draw trumps in two rounds and enjoy the diamonds.

West, however, is a wily old bird. Wary of Greek gifts, he refuses to
over-ruff and retains one more trump than dummy.

Did you back the defence? You lose, for South has a simple remedy.
He crosses to the ♠8 and leads a good diamond, throwing a heart.
Either defender, with three trumps can ruff, but neither can retain
more than one trump. Dummy's ♠10 will draw it and now the diamonds
will take care of the losing heart.

We'll end this section with three curios in which no one deceived anyone — intentionally.

A number of hands played during the past twelve months might qualify for selection as the Hand of the Year. Here is one from the distant past which remained forever the favourite of Al Sobel, one of America's greatest tournament directors, who used to make the Hand of the Year Award in the columns of the American Contract Bridge League's Monthly *Bulletin*.

Dlr. South
Love all

```
                        ♠ K 7 5 2
                        ♡ K J 7
                        ◇ 7 4
                        ♣ 8 7 5 4
        ♠ —                            ♠ J 9 4
        ♡ 10 9 8 6 4 3      N          ♡ A Q 2
        ◇ 9 5 3         W     E        ◇ K Q 10 8 6
        ♣ Q J 9 2          S           ♣ K 3
                        ♠ A Q 10 8 6 3
                        ♡ 5
                        ◇ A J 2
                        ♣ A 10 6
```

South	West	North	East
1♠	Pass	2♠	Pass
4♠	Pass	Pass	Dble.

The double was speculative, but declarer did, in fact, go one down. The remarkable feature of the hand is that West made all four tricks! It seems impossible, but this is how it happened.

West led the ♣Q and when it was allowed to hold, he switched to the ♡10. Again he was left on play. The ♣2 to East's ♣K was won by declarer, who drew trumps in three rounds and exited with a low diamond.

Coming in unexpectedly with the ◇9, West cashed the ♣J, his fourth trick.

'I wonder,' commented Al Sobel, 'if West gave his partner hell for doubling with such a trickless hand!'

Do you have misunderstandings with strange partners and suspect that such things couldn't possibly happen at the summit?

How wrong you are. A study of the records of international events would soon show that players, who have partnered each other for years, get their wires crossed as often as lesser mortals, if not more so.

Dlr. North
N/S vul.

```
                    ♠ Q 4
                    ♡ A 4
                    ◇ 10 2
                    ♣ A K Q 9 7 6 5
      ♠ A 9 6                          ♠ 8 5 3
      ♡ J 6           N                ♡ 9 7 3 2
      ◇ K Q J 8 3   W   E              ◇ 7 6 5 4
      ♣ 10 8 2        S                ♣ 4 3
                    ♠ K J 10 7 2
                    ♡ K Q 10 8 5
                    ◇ A 9
                    ♣ J
```

With the Americans sitting North-South the sequence was:

West	North	East	South
–	1♣	Pass	1♠
2◇	3◇	4◇	4NT
Pass	5♣	Pass	5◇
Pass	5♠	Pass	7♠
Dble.			

What happened?

North thought that the agreed suit was clubs. His 5♣ response to 4NT was what is known as Key Card Blackwood — the king of trumps being treated as an ace.

South believed that spades was the agreed suit and that North was showing three aces. Yes, 5♣ promised three aces or none, all very scientific.

The double of 7♠ sowed doubt in South's mind. The sight of dummy quickly removed it. What would they say at the local club if you ended up in a grand slam, missing the ace of trumps!

A difference of 4,000 match points in a match is converted to
24 IMPs (International Match-Points). That is the maximum and it is
almost as great a rarity as picking up a complete suit. A spectacular
deal in a New England tournament produced such a swing, the same
team scoring a doubled small slam in one room and a doubled grand
slam in the other.

Dlr. South
Both vul.

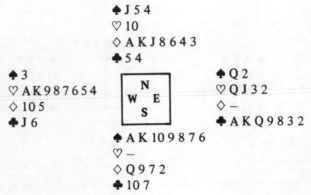

```
                        ♠ J 5 4
                        ♡ 10
                        ◇ A K J 8 6 4 3
                        ♣ 5 4
    ♠ 3                                      ♠ Q 2
    ♡ A K 9 8 7 6 5 4        N               ♡ Q J 3 2
    ◇ 10 5               W       E           ◇ —
    ♣ J 6                       S            ♣ A K Q 9 8 3 2
                        ♠ A K 10 9 8 7 6
                        ♡ —
                        ◇ Q 9 7 2
                        ♣ 10 7
```

In one room, North-South reached 6♠ after a keenly contested auction
in which diamonds had been bid and supported. East made a Lightner
double, calling for an 'unusual' lead, and duly ruffed a diamond at trick
one. A club return leads to an 800 penalty. East, however, led a heart,
so the slam was made for a score of 1660.

In the other room, East-West bid 7♡, doubled by North. Having
heard his partner open the bidding with 4♠, North decided on a 'safe'
opening and led the ◇A. Declarer spread his hand, scoring 2470.

7　*Trumps Defy the Laws of Gravity*

We've seen many difficult contracts brought home and seemingly unbreakable ones broken in the foregoing pages. We now turn to those that defy the laws of gravity, for trumps have a magic of their own and in suit contracts few things are impossible. The wizard casts his spell and a solid trick disappears, or else a winner is conjured up from nowhere. An honour is unfinessible? We'll engineer a trump coup and finesse, just the same. A bare queen is destined to fall to a hostile king? She'll side-step destiny, winning *en passant*. They have more trumps than we have? No matter. We'll score ours first, leaving theirs to ruff our losers.

But let the trumps speak for themselves and watch out for sorcery.

A spectacular setting adds interest to the best of hands, even if it owes something to the imagination.

Entitled the 'Moroccan Coup', the hand below is said to have been played in King Hassan's palace during an attempt to assassinate him.

The bidding isn't known, but the contract was 6♠.

```
              ♠ A Q 8 7
              ♡ A Q 10 9 6
              ◇ A K 7 5
              ♣ —
♠ J 10 9 6 4        ┌─────┐        ♠ —
♡ 8 5 3             │  N  │        ♡ K J 7 4 2
◇ 6              W  │     │  E     ◇ Q J 10
♣ K Q 7 6           │  S  │        ♣ 8 5 4 3 2
                    └─────┘
              ♠ K 5 3 2
              ♡ —
              ◇ 9 8 4 3 2
              ♣ A J 10 9
```

West made the obvious lead, the ♣K. Leaving out of account a bomb explosion, while the game was in progress, can the contract be made?

This is what happened.

Discarding a diamond from dummy, declarer went up with the ♣A and played the ♣J, covered and ruffed. After the ♡A and a heart ruff, South cashed his two winning clubs, throwing the ◇7 and ◇K from dummy, and led a trump. West played the ♠9 and dummy's ♠Q won. After a heart ruff, declarer crossed to the ◇A and ruffed another heart with the ♠K, West having to under-ruff. In the 3-card ending, West remained with ♠J106 under dummy's ♠A8 ♡Q.

South led a diamond and West could only score one trick. In the event, he ruffed with the ♠10 and South discarded dummy's ♡Q.

The goulash finds little favour outside France, but as we've already noted, it's still popular in Paris. Naturally freak distributions abound.

Dlr. North
E/W vul.

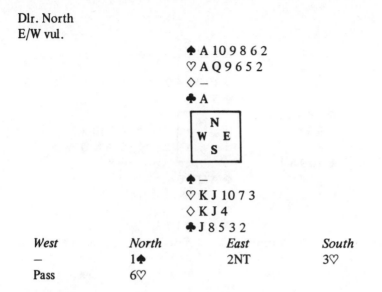

♠ A 10 9 8 6 2
♥ A Q 9 6 5 2
◇ —
♣ A

♠ —
♥ K J 10 7 3
◇ K J 4
♣ J 8 5 3 2

West	North	East	South
—	1♠	2NT	3♥
Pass	6♥		

East's 2NT is conventional, showing a two-suiter in the minors. West leads the ◇8. How should South play?

There appear to be thirteen tricks, the two black aces, and eleven tricks on a cross-ruff. And yet, they may quickly shrink to eleven if South is careless. He should ask himself: why did West, who must be shorter in clubs than in diamonds, lead the ◇8? The likeliest explanation is that he has no club and, if so, the cross-ruff won't work. West will ruff the ♣A and lead a trump.

♠ K Q J 7 5 4 3
♥ 8 3
◇ 8 7 6 2
♣ —

♠ —
♥ —
◇ A Q 10 9 5 3
♣ K Q 10 9 7 6 4

The solution is quite simple. On the ◇8 declarer throws dummy's ♣A! Now he is safe. If East has a trump to lead, the ◇K will be South's twelfth trick.

When skies are dark, declarer should assume that every cloud has a
bright silver lining, as on this deal from a Norwegian tournament.

Dlr. East
N/S vul.

```
                      ♠ K 10 4
                      ♡ K 7 6
                      ◇ 10 7 6 4 2
                      ♣ 6 2
      ♠ J 8 5 3 2        ┌─────┐        ♠ 9
      ♡ 9 5 4            │  N  │        ♡ J 10 3 2
      ◇ 8               │W   E│        ◇ A K Q J 9 5 3
      ♣ 10 9 5 4         │  S  │        ♣ 8
                        └─────┘
                      ♠ A Q 7 6
                      ♡ A Q 8
                      ◇ —
                      ♣ A K Q J 7 3
```

West	North	East	South
–	–	3NT	6♣
6◇!	Pass	Pass	6♠

The bidding isn't as exotic as it looks. East's 3NT is standard practice
these days, and shows a long, solid minor with no outside values.
Having no trick in defence himself, West rightly chooses to sacrifice in
what he knows to be his partner's suit. Even 7◇ would be cheap, but of
course West doesn't expect South to make 6♠. This is what happened.

Declarer ruffed the diamond lead and continued with the ♠K and
♠A. When East showed out, prospects were distinctly poor and yet,
with the existing distribution, the contract is unbeatable.

South cashed four clubs, then three hearts, ending in dummy, West
following all the way. That was the silver lining. At this point, declarer
had made ten tricks. A diamond, ruffed with the ♠Q, was the eleventh,
West being forced to under-ruff. Now a club, through West, up to
dummy's ♠10 ensured the twelfth, decisive trick.

Dlr. South
Love all

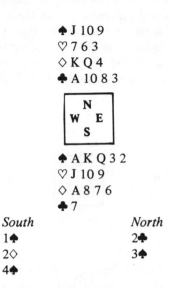

♠ J 10 9
♡ 7 6 3
◇ K Q 4
♣ A 10 8 3

♠ A K Q 3 2
♡ J 10 9
◇ A 8 7 6
♣ 7

South	North
1♠	2♣
2◇	3♠
4♠	

West leads the three top hearts, East following, and continues with the ♣5. A kibitzer, looking for a bet, asks you to lay 2-1 against the defence. Do you like the bet?

Declarer has nine top tricks, ten if diamonds break 3-3. The odds, however, are roughly 2-1 against it. A better chance is to take two rounds of trumps only before testing the diamonds. The defender who is short in diamonds may not have a trump. It's still a poor bet, but declarer can turn it into a good one through a dummy reversal.

Going up with the ♣A, he ruffs a club with the ♠A, crosses to dummy with the ♠9 and ruffs another club with the ♠K. Back in dummy with the ♠10, he ruffs the last club with his last trump, the ♠Q. Dummy is entered with the ◇Q and the ♠J draws the outstanding trump. The ◇K and ◇A bring the total to ten tricks.

♠ 8 7
♡ A K Q 4
◇ J 10 5 2
♣ 5 4 2

♠ 6 5 4
♡ 8 5 2
◇ 9 3
♣ K Q J 9 6

Bringing off coups makes one feel good, but it's not playing badly that brings in the money and match-points. Coups are too rare to affect the annual balance sheet, and the more brilliant they are, the fewer in number. Opportunities for mistakes occur hand after hand and players, who would soon find the answer to a difficult problem, often fail to solve the easy ones, precisely because they are easy and seem to pose no problem, as here:

Dlr. North
E/W vul.

```
            ♠ 3                            ♠ A J 7 4 2
            ♡ J 10 9 8 7 6      N          ♡ A Q
            ◇ K 2          W        E       ◇ A 10 7 6 5
            ♣ A 7 6 5          S           ♣ J
```

North	East	South	West
3♣	Dble.	Pass	4♡

North led the ♣K, South following with the two. West won, ruffed a club with the ♡Q and . . . But it was already too late. South over-ruffed with the ♡K and the trump return killed the unbeatable contract stone dead. All West had to do was to ruff a club with the ♡A, get back with ◇K and ruff another club with the ♡Q. Whether or not South over-ruffed with the ♡K West could be sure of eleven tricks. Couldn't North ruff a diamond return? Hardly. With a singleton diamond that would have been his lead. Was West then a bad player? Not really. It was just that the hand was too easy for him. Now had it needed a coup . . .

If you remove partner's double at the five level, you must be prepared to do one of two things — to make your contract or prove that opponents would have made theirs. Such was South's predicament here.

Dlr. East
Both vul.

```
                      ♠ A K J
                      ♡ 9 6 3
                      ◇ A Q J 4
                      ♣ K J 10
    ♠ Q                                      ♠ 7
    ♡ A J 10 7 5       ┌─────────┐           ♡ Q 8
    ◇ 6 5              │    N    │           ◇ K 10 9 8 7
    ♣ 6 5 4 3 2        │ W     E │           ♣ A Q 9 8 7
                       │    S    │
                       └─────────┘
                      ♠ 10 9 8 6 5 4 3 2
                      ♡ K 4 2
                      ◇ 3 2
                      ♣ —
```

West	North	East	South
—	—	1◇	Pass
1♡	Dble.	2♣	4♠
5♣	Dble.	Pass	5♠

West led the ◇6 and South could see four losers, a diamond and three hearts. Could he make two of them disappear?

Going up with dummy's ◇A, he led the ♣K, intending to throw his second diamond if East played low. When East covered, South ruffed and, crossing to the table with a trump, he led the ♣J. Again East covered and South ruffed.

Returning to dummy with a trump, South cashed the ♣10, getting rid, at last, of his second diamond, and continued with the ◇Q to bring off yet another ruffing finesse. Dummy's third trump was an entry to the ◇J, South's eleventh trick.

It's true that West might have had one of the club honours or even the ◇K, but then East would have needed the ♡A for his bid and the result would have been the same.

There are plays more difficult technically than the Grand Coup, but none more spectacular.

This example is taken from *Bridge d'Italia*.

Dlr. South
Love all

```
                    ♠ A
                    ♡ A K Q J
                    ◇ A K Q 2
                    ♣ A K 3 2
        ♠ —                        ♠ Q 10 6 4
        ♡ 8 5 4 3 2      N         ♡ 10 9 7 6
        ◇ 9 4 3       W     E      ◇ J 10 6
        ♣ J 10 9 8 7     S         ♣ Q 6
                    ♠ K J 9 8 7 5 3 2
                    ♡ —
                    ◇ 8 7 5
                    ♣ 5 4
```

South	West	North	East
4♠	Pass	7♠	Dble.

By bidding 5NT, the grand slam force, North could have found out that South was missing one of the three top honours.

With thirty points, more than he had ever had in his life, he didn't bother to investigate.

East's double was inexcusable and from the first South played him for the four missing trumps. Since he couldn't finesse, he would shorten his trumps to East's level, then lead from dummy. Fortunately, entries were plentiful.

Trick one went to the ♣A and trick two was a heart ruff. Crossing three times to the ◇AKQ South ruffed three more hearts.

Then came the ♣K and dummy's last diamond. With trumps only left, East had to ruff. Over-ruffing, South went over to the ♠A and led a club. At this point he had left the ♠KJ and East the ♣Q10 — and it was East's turn to play.

Trumps having been shortened four times, it was a quadruple Grand Coup.

Richard Lederer, Britain's 'Mr Bridge' during the great Culbertsonian era, used to say: 'Weak players shouldn't double.' The corollary is that it's wise to think twice before doubling strong players. Here's a case in point, reported in the South African *Bridge Bulletin*.

Dlr. West
Love all

```
                    ♠ A 10 6 2
                    ♡ A J 2
                    ◇ 9 8
                    ♣ A Q 4 2
    ♠ K 8 3                          ♠ Q J 7 5 4
    ♡ Q 6 5          N               ♡ 10 8 4 3
    ◇ A Q 10 7 4   W   E             ◇ –
    ♣ J 5            S               ♣ K 10 9 8
                    ♠ 9
                    ♡ K 9 7
                    ◇ K J 6 5 3 2
                    ♣ 7 6 3
```

West	North	East	South
1NT	Dble.	2♠	3◇
Dble.			

West led the ♣J, the finesse losing to East's ♣K. The ♣10 came back and South took stock. What made West double? Holding the ♠KQ he would have led the ♠K. He didn't have the ♣K either. So he had a minimum opening and therefore five diamonds to justify his double. South played accordingly.

Winning the second trick with the ♣A, he laid down the ♠A and ruffed a spade. Then came the ♡K, a heart to dummy's ♡J and another spade ruff. That came to six tricks. The ♡A was the seventh. On dummy's last spade South threw his third club. Having trumps only left, despite his ◇AQ107 over South's ◇KJ65, he had to concede two tricks — and the contract.

Dlr. South
Both vul.

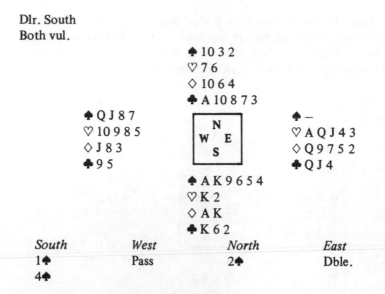

```
                    ♠ 10 3 2
                    ♡ 7 6
                    ◇ 10 6 4
                    ♣ A 10 8 7 3
   ♠ Q J 8 7                           ♠ —
   ♡ 10 9 8 5         N                ♡ A Q J 4 3
   ◇ J 8 3         W     E             ◇ Q 9 7 5 2
   ♣ 9 5              S                ♣ Q J 4
                    ♠ A K 9 6 5 4
                    ♡ K 2
                    ◇ A K
                    ♣ K 6 2
```

South	West	North	East
1♠	Pass	2♠	Dble.
4♠			

West leads the ♡10 to East's ♡A. The ♡Q comes back.

Which side shall we back? Declarer or defenders? Having lost one
trick, declarer, it seems, must lose three more, two trumps and a club.

Quite right, South will win, for if the answer were obvious the
question wouldn't be put in the first place.

This hand came up in an American tournament. South's first move,
when he laid down the ♠A and discovered the 4-0 trump break, was to
cash the ◇AK. Then he crossed to the ♣A, ruffed a diamond, cashed
the ♣K and exited with a low trump, carefully throwing dummy's
♠10 under West's ♠J.

If, at this point, West returns a heart, South ruffs in dummy and
discards his losing club.

If West returns a trump, he won't make his ♠Q — but only because
the ♠10 no longer blocks the suit in dummy. Otherwise East would win
the next trick, necessarily a club, and a diamond through South would
allow West, playing after him, to score his bare ♠Q.

Hungary has produced some of the world's greatest card players and though little has been heard of bridge in Hungary since the war, there are now unmistakable signs of a revival.

One of the big trophies is the Mecsek Cup. Staged at the annual tournament in Pecs, the event attracts competitors from Austria, Czechoslovakia and Poland.

This was a grand slam bid and made by the winning team from Budapest.

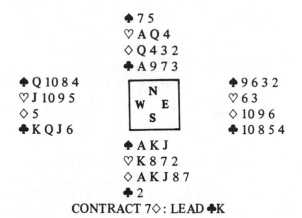

♠ 7 5
♡ A Q 4
◇ Q 4 3 2
♣ A 9 7 3

♠ Q 10 8 4
♡ J 10 9 5
◇ 5
♣ K Q J 6

♠ 9 6 3 2
♡ 6 3
◇ 10 9 6
♣ 10 8 5 4

♠ A K J
♡ K 8 7 2
◇ A K J 8 7
♣ 2

CONTRACT 7◇: LEAD ♣K

How should South play? He has eleven top tricks and if trumps break 2-2, he can score two more by ruffing in dummy. Alternatively, if trumps are 3-1, a 3-3 heart break or a spade finesse would make up for it. Here nothing works. Is there any other way?

The Hungarian declarer went up with the ♣A and at trick two ruffed a club — the key play. After laying down the ◇AK he crossed to the ♡Q, then to the ♡A and ruffed two more clubs. Next came the ♠AK and a spade ruff. The ◇Q on which South threw his ♡2 now removed East's last trump and the ♡K scored the thirteenth trick.

Dlr. South
Both vul.

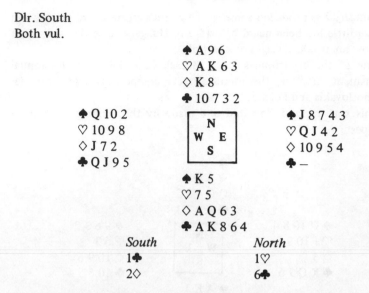

```
                         ♠ A 9 6
                         ♡ A K 6 3
                         ◇ K 8
                         ♣ 10 7 3 2
        ♠ Q 10 2              N              ♠ J 8 7 4 3
        ♡ 10 9 8         W         E         ♡ Q J 4 2
        ◇ J 7 2               S             ◇ 10 9 5 4
        ♣ Q J 9 5                            ♣ —
                         ♠ K 5
                         ♡ 7 5
                         ◇ A Q 6 3
                         ♣ A K 8 6 4
```

South	*North*
1♣	1♡
2◇	6♣

It's a good contract and a reasonable, if unscientific, method of reaching it. Hearing South's reverse, North knows that he has all the right cards and his only fear is that a cold grand slam may be missed.

The distribution is unkind and comes to light at trick two, when, after winning the heart lead, South plays a club and East shows out. The contract, however, can still be made. How should declarer play?

South goes up with the ♣A and plans to strip West of all but trumps, then to throw him in.

Crossing to the ♡K he ruffs a heart and continues with the ♠K, ♠A and a spade ruff. Three rounds of diamonds come next, and when West follows all the way, the stage is set for the *coup de grace* — the fourth diamond.

What West does is immaterial. If he ruffs low, he is over-ruffed. If he ruffs high, he will have to lead a trump away from his Q(J) and nine of clubs.

Dlr. South
Love all

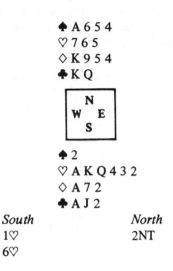

♠ A 6 5 4
♡ 7 6 5
◇ K 9 5 4
♣ K Q

♠ 2
♡ A K Q 4 3 2
◇ A 7 2
♣ A J 2

South	North
1♡	2NT
6♡	

Old-fashioned Acol. Scientists could take another four rounds of bidding to reach this excellent slam — or to stop en route, maybe, in some subtle cue-bid. The point of the hand, however, is in the play.

West leads the ♡J and East throws the ♣3. Very unlucky. Is there still hope? South has two inescapable losers, a trump and a diamond, and the only chance is to lose both at once. For this to be possible, West must have the right distribution. At trick two, South crosses to the ♠A and ruffs a spade. Going over to the ♣K, then to the ♣Q, he ruffs two more spades, hoping that all follow — East, too, for he doesn't want West to have five spades. Next he cashes his winners, the ♡AKQ, the ◇AK and the ♣A. If West follows, all is well.

♠ K J 7 3
♡ J 10 9 8
◇ Q 8
♣ 9 7 5

♠ Q 10 9 8
♡ –
◇ J 10 6 3
♣ 10 8 6 4 3

South has made twelve tricks. His last card, the ◇2, falls on West's master trump.

After two passes, East, on your right, bids 7♡. They are vulnerable and you are not. What do you do with: ♠ AJ97 ♡5 ◇72 ♣AQJ1076?

That was the problem facing England international Claude Rodrigue during a rubber at the St James's Club.

'What would you have done?' asked Claude.

Before committing myself, I asked him to name East, for faces alter cases. If East is an optimist who might take chances against say, a 4-1 trump break, I would pass ... Against a solid bidder, 7♠ would be a cheap sacrifice. This was the deal.

```
                    ♠ Q 6 5 2
                    ♡ 7 6 3
                    ◇ 8 4
                    ♣ K 9 5 3
   ♠ K 10 8 4 3                        ♠ —
   ♡ 10 8 4        ┌──────────┐        ♡ A K Q J 9 2
   ◇ J 3          │    N     │        ◇ A K Q J 10 9 6 5
   ♣ 8 4 2        │ W     E  │        ♣ —
                   │    S     │
                   └──────────┘
                    ♠ A J 9 7
                    ♡ 5
                    ◇ 7 2
                    ♣ A Q J 10 7 6
```

West	North	East	South
Pass	Pass	7♡	7♠
Dble.			

East took the ◇AK and the ♡K. Then Rodrigue ruffed a heart. Knowing that East had no black card, he carefully refrained from touching trumps. No defence could prevent him from scoring his four trumps, dummy's ♠Q and three clubs, a 900 penalty against 2510 for a vulnerable grand slam.

In view of East's honours, Rodrigue would have made 10 points profit had he taken no trick at all — not even the ♠A!

If you make 7♠ on the hand below, you are to be congratulated. If you fail, you can take comfort in the thought that two great players did likewise when the deal came up in an international match some years ago.

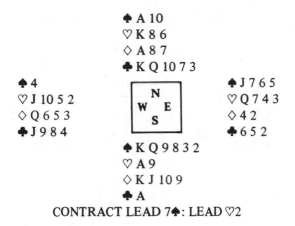

♠ A 10
♡ K 8 6
◇ A 8 7
♣ K Q 10 7 3

♠ 4
♡ J 10 5 2
◇ Q 6 5 3
♣ J 9 8 4

♠ J 7 6 5
♡ Q 7 4 3
◇ 4 2
♣ 6 5 2

♠ K Q 9 8 3 2
♡ A 9
◇ K J 10 9
♣ A

CONTRACT LEAD 7♠: LEAD ♡2

How should South play?

This is what happened. Winning trick one with the ♡A, both declarers led a trump to the ♠A, then the ♠10. West showed out and it was too late to do anything about it.

A 4-1 trump break being the only danger, declarer should give it his entire attention. After the ♡A should come the ♣A, then the ♠K and only then the ♠A, revealing the position.

To catch the ♠J declarer shortens his trumps twice, so as to have no more than East. Since he must ruff two clubs, sacrificing a winner, he now needs the diamond finesse. So, after ruffing a club at trick five, he leads the ◇J, then, if West doesn't cover, the ◇10 to dummy's ace. Next South throws the ◇9 on the ♣K and ruffs a club. Crossing to the ♡K he remains with ♠Q9 ◇K poised over East's ♠J7 ♡Q, and the lead is in dummy.

The ♣Q is played.

If spectacular coups come up too rarely to be materially rewarding, they make up for it by the pleasure they give psychologically.

Declarer in a ladies international match was entitled to a thrill here:

Dlr. West
Love all

```
                        ♠ 9 3
                        ♡ A K 6 3
                        ◇ K Q
                        ♣ A K 10 4 3
        ♠ J 10 4 2                          ♠ K 8 6
        ♡ 10              ┌─────────┐        ♡ Q 8 7 2
        ◇ J 9 8 6 3      │   N     │        ◇ 7 4 2
        ♣ Q J 5          │ W   E   │        ♣ 9 8 2
                         │   S     │
                         └─────────┘
                        ♠ A Q 7 5
                        ♡ J 9 5 4
                        ◇ A 10 5
                        ♣ 7 6
```

North	South
1♣	1♡
4♡	4♠
6♡	

West led the ♠2. Had trumps broken kindly, the hand would have presented no problem. Declarer would take two rounds of trumps and ruff two spades in dummy, not minding if East over-ruffed.

After the ♠A, the ♠Q and a spade ruff, came the ♡AK, revealing the 4-1 break. That called for a change of plan.

Declarer cashed the ◇KQ, laid down the ♣AK and continued with another club. The 3-3 club break was against the odds, but it didn't matter either way for West could do no harm. When East followed, South ruffed with the ♡9 and now came the key play, the ◇A was ruffed in dummy and a club followed. No matter what East did — he was left with ♡Q8 — declarer's bare ♡J would bring in the twelfth trick.

Dlr. North
N/S vul.

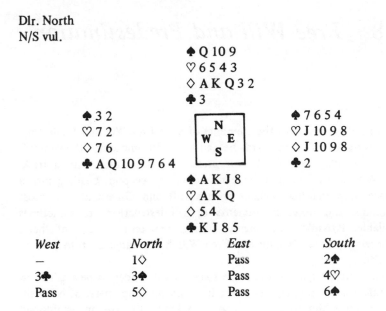

```
                    ♠ Q 10 9
                    ♡ 6 5 4 3
                    ◇ A K Q 3 2
                    ♣ 3
     ♠ 3 2                           ♠ 7 6 5 4
     ♡ 7 2          N                ♡ J 10 9 8
     ◇ 7 6        W   E              ◇ J 10 9 8
     ♣ A Q 10 9 7 6 4    S           ♣ 2
                    ♠ A K J 8
                    ♡ A K Q
                    ◇ 5 4
                    ♣ K J 8 5
```

West	North	East	South
—	1◇	Pass	2♠
3♣	3♠	Pass	4♡
Pass	5◇	Pass	6♠

West opened a trump. Winning in dummy, declarer led a club to his ♣J and West's ♣Q. Another trump came back. Declarer took it in his hand and ruffed a club in dummy.

Two junior kibitzers exchanged views.

'That killing trump lead and continuation will keep him to eleven tricks,' said the first.

'Don't you believe it,' rejoined the second J.K. 'Can't you see East squirming? He can't part with a diamond, and if he throws a heart, dummy's fourth heart will be South's twelfth trick.'

Which of the two kibitzers was right?

While East is tossed from horn to horn of his dilemma, there is time to weigh up the situation.

Ready?

The second J.K. was right — up to a point. Whether East discards a diamond or a heart, declarer will make his contract. But East doesn't have to throw a red card. He can 'discard' a trump! And now the contract is unmakable, for East plays after dummy and he will know what to keep when seven cards only remain.

8 *Free Will and Predestination*

An End Play combines the elements of both Free Will and Predestination. Stripped of all the cards he can lead with impunity, the victim is forced to play one which will present his tormentor with a trick. Hara-kiri is his fate, but he can choose his weapon. Leading into a tenace or presenting declarer with a ruff and discard are the most common. But other instruments of self-destruction are sometimes available. Providing the enemy with a vital entry is one of them. Squeezing partner is another. Free Will has a large part to play in the ritual.

The better his hand, the more likely is a defender to be singled out by fate for an end-play. To avert it, to keep a step ahead of Nemesis, may require him to jettison aces and kings, to give up established winners and, on occasion, to get rid of superfluous trumps by uder-ruffing. When pressure mounts it is often right to play partner for a card or cards he may not have. The risk cannot be avoided. Similarly, if to discard deceptively requires an honour to be unguarded, there must be no hesitation, no squirming. And it must be done early. If fate is to be thwarted, there is no time to lose.

'Could I do more than give myself an 80 per cent chance?' asked the Professor rhetorically.

'You might have tried 100 per cent,' suggested the Senior Kibitzer.

Dlr. South
Love all

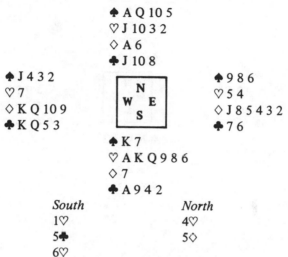

	South	North
	1♡	4♡
	5♣	5◊
	6♡	

West led the ◊K to dummy's ◊A. The Professor drew trumps in two rounds and turned to the spades, hoping to bring down the ♠J. No one obliged, so he ran the ♣J losing to West's ♣Q. The ♠J came back.

The Professor ruffed and crossing to dummy with a trump, ran the ♣10. When that, too, failed he bewailed his fate.

'I win if the club honours are split, as they should be, or if East has both or if the ♠J comes down. The odds are ...'

'Very likely,' agreed S.K. hastily. 'But the odds are quite irrelevant. So why worry about them? Ruff dummy's ◊6 at trick two, draw trumps and lead out the spades, ruffing the last one.

'Now at last, having stripped the hand, you cross with a trump and run the ♣J, West must either lead into your ♣A9 or present you with a ruff and discard.'

In textbooks brilliant plays are invariably crowned with success. At the card table, brilliance isn't always enough. If one side plays well, so can the other. Which one will get the upper hand here?

Dlr. South
Love all

```
                        ♠ A 4
                        ♡ 8 5 3
                        ◇ 9 8 7 6
                        ♣ K J 9 4
      ♠ J 10 9 8 7 6        ┌─────────┐        ♠ 5
      ♡ 10 6 4 2            │    N    │        ♡ J 9 7
      ◇ Q                   │ W     E │        ◇ K J 10 5 3
      ♣ A 3                 │    S    │        ♣ Q 10 8 7
                           └─────────┘
                        ♠ K Q 3 2
                        ♡ A K Q
                        ◇ A 4 2
                        ♣ 6 5 2
```

South	West	North	East
1♣	1♠	2♣	2◇
3NT			

West led the ◇Q. East couldn't overtake without risk of promoting dummy's ◇9 and at trick two West switched to a spade. Winning in hand, declarer led a club, inserting the ♣J and losing to East's ♣Q. The ◇K came next and West discarded — the ♣A!

Bearing in mind South's deceptive 1♣ bid and placing him with four clubs, West was creating an entry for East's diamonds.

Despite this gift, declarer still had no more than eight tricks, but he could place every card and that was enough. He cashed his winners in the majors, East coming down to the ◇J10 and ♣108. Now a diamond forced him to lead a club into dummy's ♣K9.

Dlr. North
Love all

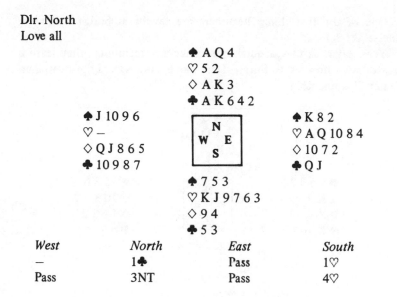

♠ A Q 4
♡ 5 2
◇ A K 3
♣ A K 6 4 2

♠ J 10 9 6
♡ –
◇ Q J 8 6 5
♣ 10 9 8 7

♠ K 8 2
♡ A Q 10 8 4
◇ 10 7 2
♣ Q J

♠ 7 5 3
♡ K J 9 7 6 3
◇ 9 4
♣ 5 3

West	North	East	South
–	1♣	Pass	1♡
Pass	3NT	Pass	4♡

West leads the ♠J. Do we back declarer or the defence?

Sitting South, when this hand came up, was Dorothy Hayden, now Mrs Alan Truscott, wife of the British-born bridge editor of the *New York Times* and the world's top-ranking woman player at the time of writing.

Reasoning that West was unlikely to have led away from the ♠K, Dorothy went up with dummy's ♠A and finessed the ♡9. West's void was a shock, but all wasn't yet lost. Declarer crossed to dummy with a club and led a second trump. East rose with the ♡A and returned a club. Dorothy ruffed a club, cashed the ◇AK and continued with another club.

East, at this stage, holds: ♠K8 ♡Q108. If he discards the ♣8, he is thrown in with the ♠K and forced to lead a trump into the ♡KJ. In the event, East ruffed with the ♡8. Dorothy over-ruffed, cashed the ♡K and threw East in with a heart, forcing a spade lead up to dummy.

East's freedom of action was restricted to choice of weapons — for his own destruction.

One of the first things beginners are taught at bridge is how to finesse.

Years later, as they acquire experience and technique, they learn a greater art — how not to finesse. Here's an example from the Australian Teams Championships.

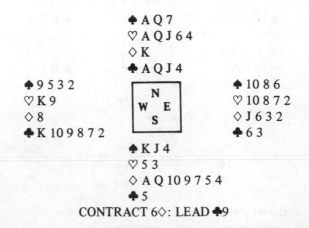

CONTRACT 6◇: LEAD ♣9

Declarer was Australian star Roelof Smilde. He went up with the ♣A, cashed the ◇K and entering the closed hand with the ♠J, took two more rounds of trumps.

When West showed out, a trump loser became inevitable and the contract seemingly hinged on a successful heart finesse or else a ruffing finesse in clubs.

Which should it be? The wrong guess would, of course, spell defeat. Smilde found a way of avoiding all guesswork. He crossed to the ♠Q and ruffed a club. Then, going back to the ♠A, he ruffed another club.

When East showed out, he threw him in with a trump. Had East had a fourth spade, Smilde would have had to take the heart finesse.

As it was, East had to lead a heart and all was well.

Dlr. West
Love all

```
            ♠ Q J 8 7 5
            ♡ A Q
            ◇ A K J
            ♣ K Q J

              N
            W   E
              S

            ♠ A 10 9 6 4 3
            ♡ 7 6
            ◇ 10 5 3
            ♣ A 10
```

North	South
2♣	2♠
3♠	4♣
4◇	4♠
5♡	5♠
6♠	

As soon as North hears South's 2♠ a slam is bound to be reached. Could it be a grand slam?

Unlikely. Even after South's cue-bid of 4♣, too much is missing. The 5NT Grand Slam Force, would clear up the trump position, but question marks would remain over the red suits. So, when South has no more to say, North settles for 6♠.

West leads the ◇9 to dummy's ◇A. On the ♠Q East plays the ♠2. What are South's chances.

There is practically nothing between finessing and playing for the drop of the ♠K, and, of course, the red suit finesses may both be wrong. For all that, the slam is unbreakable. South goes up with the ♠A, and if the ♠K doesn't drop, he cashes his clubs, then he throws East in with the ♠K.

```
    ♠ —                          ♠ K 2
    ♡ J 9 8 4 3 2     N          ♡ K 10 5
    ◇ 9 8 2        W     E       ◇ Q 7 6 4
    ♣ 7 6 3 2         S          ♣ 9 8 5 4
```

Whatever East returns, presents South with his twelfth trick.

It was one of those days when everything was going wrong.

Dlr. South
Love all

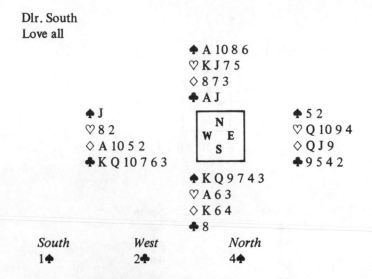

               ♠ A 10 8 6
               ♡ K J 7 5
               ◇ 8 7 3
               ♣ A J

♠ J   ♠ 5 2
♡ 8 2   N   ♡ Q 10 9 4
◇ A 10 5 2   W E   ◇ Q J 9
♣ K Q 10 7 6 3   S   ♣ 9 5 4 2

               ♠ K Q 9 7 4 3
               ♡ A 6 3
               ◇ K 6 4
               ♣ 8

South	*West*	*North*
1♠	2♣	4♠

West led the ♣K and South surveyed his dubious prospects. On the bidding, West surely had the ◇A, so everything would hinge on the ♡Q, and was he likely to bring off a finesse?

Suddenly he had an inspiration.

He would make his contract no matter who had what.

How did South play? Any ideas?

There was one card he could place with certainty, the ♣Q, and that was enough. Going up with the ♣A, he drew trumps, cashed the ♡A, then the ♡K and continued with the ♣J, throwing his third heart. Let West do his worst.

A diamond up to South's ◇K or a club, conceding a ruff and discard, would cost West a trick. If he had a heart — or both hearts — it wouldn't help him. Declarer would go up with dummy's ♡J and either it would win, or else East would have the ♡Q. Then South would ruff and score dummy's last heart, for now the suit would have broken 3-3.

Who is going to win on this deal, reported in the *Revue Francaise de Bridge*?

Dlr. West
N/S vul.

```
                         ♠ K 10 5
                         ♡ K 9 7 5
                         ◇ J 4 2
                         ♣ J 7 3
        ♠ 9 3 2                              ♠ J 8 7 6
        ♡ Q J 10 3        N                  ♡ 8 6 4
        ◇ A Q 8 6      W     E               ◇ 9 3
        ♣ K 8             S                  ♣ 10 9 5 2
                         ♠ A Q 4
                         ♡ A 2
                         ◇ K 10 7 5
                         ♣ A Q 6 4
```

West	North	East	South
1◇	Pass	Pass	Dble.
Pass	1♡	Pass	2NT
Pass	3NT		

With 27 points and three stoppers in every suit, all should be plain-sailing. West, however, is a wily player and, knowing that dummy will have four hearts, he leads the ♡3. Declarer plays low from dummy and wins East's ♡8 with his ♡A. The third heart stopper has disappeared.

Coming in with the ♣K at trick two, West clears his hearts and South still has only eight tricks — three spades, two hearts and three clubs. And he cannot afford to lose two diamonds to set one up, for defenders would then have five tricks.

Is South going down?

By no means, for that wily West is about to be *hoist on his own petard*. Declarer cashes his six winners in spades and clubs and exits with a heart. West scores the trick for which he has fought so hard, but being thrown in with it, must now lead a diamond, presenting South with his ninth trick.

Declarer on the hand below was the Belgian master Charles Monk, playing in a top-class pairs event.

Dlr. West
N/S vul.

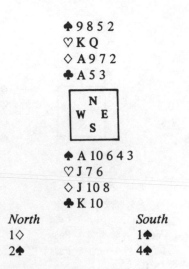

```
              ♠ 9 8 5 2
              ♡ K Q
              ◇ A 9 7 2
              ♣ A 5 3

                 N
              W     E
                 S

              ♠ A 10 6 4 3
              ♡ J 7 6
              ◇ J 10 8
              ♣ K 10
```

North	South
1◇	1♠
2♣	4♠

West leads the ♡A, then the ♡3, East following in ascending order. How should South play?

Assuming that trumps break 2-2 – or there's no hope – two finesses in diamonds lose only when East has both honours. Excellent odds.

Monk, however, preferred a certainty – barring unforeseeable ruffs. He cashed the ♣A and ♣K, discarded dummy's ♣5 on his ♡J and led out the ♠A and ♠3.

```
♠ Q 7              N           ♠ K J
♡ A 10 8 5 2   W      E        ♡ 9 4 3
◇ 3                S           ◇ K Q 6 5 4
♣ Q J 8 7 6                    ♣ 9 4 2
```

No matter which defender wins the second trump, and even though East has both diamond honours, declarer will only lose one diamond.

'Every card wrong. The odds against this fiendish distribution must be at least 10-1,' fumed the Professor.

'Very likely,' agreed the Senior Kibitzer, 'but you still had better than a 50-50 chance.'

Dlr. West
E/W vul.

```
                    ♠ J 8
                    ♡ K J 6
                    ◇ A K 7 5
                    ♣ K 7 6 5
  ♠ K 10 9 7 6 4         N         ♠ Q 5 3 2
  ♡ 3 2              W       E     ♡ A Q
  ◇ Q 10 6 2             S         ◇ J 9 4
  ♣ J                               ♣ Q 10 9 8
                    ♠ A
                    ♡ 10 9 8 7 5 4
                    ◇ 8 3
                    ♣ A 4 3 2
```

North	South
1◇	1♡
2♣	3♣
3♡	4♡

West led the ♡3. East took his two trump tricks and exited with a spade.

The Professor cashed three more trumps, hoping for a helpful discard, and broached the clubs. Finding them 4-1, he had to concede defeat.

'Instead of inveighing against your bad luck,' observed SK coldly, 'you would have done better to take advantage of your good luck, the 2-2 trump break.

'After the ♠A, at trick three, you go to the ◇K and ruff the ♠J. Next you cross to the ◇A and ruff a diamond. The ♣A and ♣K follow and the 4-1 break comes to light, but you are ready for it. You lead dummy's fourth diamond and discard a club. Unless the same defender, East in this case, is long in both minors, he must present you with a ruff and discard, your tenth trick.'

Dlr. West
Love all

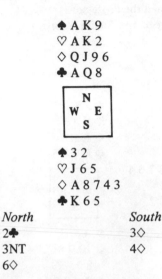

♠ A K 9
♡ A K 2
◇ Q J 9 6
♣ A Q 8

♠ 3 2
♡ J 6 5
◇ A 8 7 4 3
♣ K 6 5

North	South
2♣	3◇
3NT	4◇
6◇	

The bidding is straightforward. North's 3NT rebid shows a balanced hand and a minimum 2♣ opening. South looks for better things and North is happy to bid the slam.

West leads the ♡8. Declarer goes up with the ♡A and runs the ◇Q, which holds. The ◇J is covered by East's ◇K and West shows out.

What are declarer's prospects?

Assuming a normal lead, he can hardly lose. After the ◇A, he cashes his ♠AK and ruffs a spade. Next he plays off his clubs, not caring whether or not East follows. If he ruffs, he will have to lead a heart, away from his queen, or a spade, conceding a ruff and discard. If East has three clubs, declarer will throw him in with the ◇10 and it will come to the same thing.

♠ J 6 5 4
♡ 8 7 4
◇ 5
♣ J 10 7 3 2

♠ Q 10 8 7
♡ Q 10 9 3
◇ K 10 2
♣ 9 4

Declarer would doubtless play the same way on any lead, but West's ♡8 clearly suggests that East has the ♡Q and that points the way.

'I like hands that require a bit of play,' said South to his Guardian Angel. 'If, however, every card that matters is invariably wrong, there's no fun in it. Now other people . . .'

The G.A. waved his magic wand.

Dlr. West
Love all

```
                        ♠ K 6 4
                        ♡ Q 8 5
                        ◇ A 10 3
                        ♣ K J 10 5
     ♠ J 10 8                          ♠ A Q 9 7 5 3 2
     ♡ J 10 9 2        N               ♡ K 6 3
     ◇ J 8 7 6 2    W     E            ◇ 9 4
     ♣ 7              S                 ♣ 4
                        ♠ —
                        ♡ A 7 4
                        ◇ K Q 5
                        ♣ A Q 9 8 6 3 2
```

West	North	East	South
Pass	1NT	2♠	3♣
Pass	3NT	Pass	4♣
Pass	4◇	Pass	6♣

West led the ♠J. It was apparent to South that the contract would hinge on the position of the ♡K, and in view of East's bid, he was likely to have it. And yet, for once, with G.A.'s help, he might have a little luck. So, after five rounds of trumps and three rounds of diamonds, he led the ♡A, then the ♡4. One down.

A chord snapped on the magic harp, a wing flapped angrily and the scales fell from South's eyes.

After the opening lead, the contract was unbreakable. All South had to do, after drawing trumps, was to ruff dummy's low spade, cash the three diamonds and lead the ♠K, throwing on it a heart. East couldn't avoid conceding a ruff and discard or leading away from his ♡K.

Dlr. West
Love all

```
                    ♠ 10 8 7 5 3
                    ♡ 7 6 5 3 2
                    ◇ A
                    ♣ 3 2
                  ┌───────┐
                  │   N   │
                  │ W   E │
                  │   S   │
                  └───────┘
                    ♠ K 6
                    ♡ K J
                    ◇ K Q J 10 5
                    ♣ K J 10 9
```

West	North	East	South
1♣	Pass	Pass	Dble.
Pass	1♡	Pass	1NT

West leads the ♣5. East wins with the ♣A and returns the ♣7. How should South play?

Since East, who couldn't keep 1♣ open, has found an ace, he can certainly have no other high card. Declarer must assume, therefore, that West has both the missing aces and the ♣Q.

He has seven tricks, if he can get at them — five diamonds and two clubs, after conceding a trick to the ♣Q. Unfortunately, the diamonds are blocked and there's no entry to the South hand.

The answer is to go up with the ♣K at trick two and play the ♣J, jettisoning dummy's ◇A! Now the diamonds have been unblocked and whatever West returns, South will win in his hand.

```
    ♠ A Q              ┌───────┐        ♠ J 9 4 2
    ♡ A Q 9 4          │   N   │        ♡ 10 8
    ◇ 9 6 3            │ W   E │        ◇ 8 7 4 2
    ♣ Q 8 6 5          │   S   │        ♣ A 7 4
                       └───────┘
```

If West returns a club or a diamond, declarer will make seven tricks at least, probably eight on an endplay. A spade or heart return will make the eighth trick a certainty.

The hand below came up in a tournament in the U.S.

Dlr. East
Both vul.

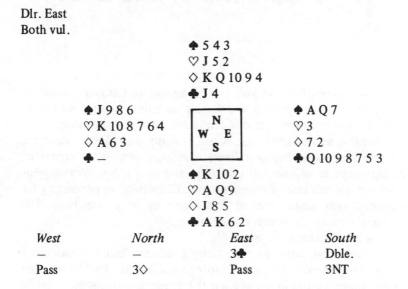

```
            ♠ 5 4 3
            ♡ J 5 2
            ◇ K Q 10 9 4
            ♣ J 4
♠ J 9 8 6        N        ♠ A Q 7
♡ K 10 8 7 6 4  W   E     ♡ 3
◇ A 6 3          S        ◇ 7 2
♣ —                       ♣ Q 10 9 8 7 5 3
            ♠ K 10 2
            ♡ A Q 9
            ◇ J 8 5
            ♣ A K 6 2
```

West	North	East	South
–	–	3♣	Dble.
Pass	3◇	Pass	3NT

West leads the ♡7. The reader can treat it as a double-dummy problem. How can South make 3NT?

The first move is to win trick one with the ♡Q, not the ♡9, leaving the ♡J as a possible entry to dummy. Declarer leads diamonds and West, needless to say, holds up his ◇A till the third round. He returns a spade to East's ♠A on which South, thinking ahead, drops his ♠10. He wins the spade return with the ♠K and exits with the ♠2. He's home!

If West wins, he can cash his fourth spade, but must then lead a heart to dummy's ♡J. If East wins, he must lead a club to dummy's ♣J. Either way, declarer has an entry to two good diamonds.

Note that if South fails to jettison his ♠10, West can refuse to win the third spade, leaving declarer on play, one trick short of his contract.

9   *Department of Bad Luck*

Do your finesses fail? Do you run up against bad trump breaks? In short, are you unlucky? If so, there's something wrong with your game, for luck is a technique that can be mastered like any other.

Common sense, rather than science, is the prerequisite. Reaching sophisticated slams, bringing home seemingly impossible contracts, daring coups in defence, all exhilarate and excite, but occasions for brilliance are too rare to ensure success. Conversely, opportunities for mistakes, quite simple ones at that, come up hand after hand. The player who makes the fewest is the winner.

How are mistakes to be avoided?

Concentration, attention, forethought, all the deadly virtues come into it, but the most effective antidote to bad luck is a healthy measure of pessimism. Just as in the auction the opener selects his bid in readiness for partner's most awkward response, so in the play the first step should be to look for the murky cloud that hovers over the silver lining. Unlike standard safety plays, the mechanics of playing safely call for improvisaiton and cannot be memorised. Each problem must be solved as it comes up, each situation treated strictly on its demerits.

More than once already the reader has met the Professor. You are about to see more of him, for we are entering the Department of Bad Luck and the Professor has all the attributes of the unlucky player. Conversant with the odds and the percentages, familiar with learned theses and savant stratagems, he is weak on horse sense and suffers from that fatal malady — the knack of doing the right thing at the wrong time.

New gadgets and conventions – some good, some bad – come into being almost daily, but good play remains the same throughout the years. Declarer on this week's hand – which goes back half a century – was Josephine Culbertson.

Dlr. North
Love all

```
                        ♠ A 10
                        ♡ K Q 7
                        ◇ A K 8 6 4 3
                        ♣ 9 5
        ♠ K Q J 9 6 3         ┌──────────┐        ♠ 8 5 4 2
        ♡ J 10 9             │    N     │        ♡ 8
        ◇ 10 7              │ W     E  │        ◇ Q J 9 5
        ♣ Q 8               │    S     │        ♣ K J 10 4
                            └──────────┘
                        ♠ 7
                        ♡ A 6 5 4 3 2
                        ◇ 2
                        ♣ A 7 6 3 2
```

West	North	East	South
–	1◇	Pass	1♡
1♠	3◇	3♠	4♣
Pass	4NT	Pass	5NT
Pass	6♡		

Easley Blackwood was still to devise his ace-finding convention, and Culbertson's 4-5NT held undisputed sway. North's 4NT promised two aces and the king of a bid suit. Josephine's 5NT response showed two aces.

West led the ♠K. How should the play proceed?

Setting up the clubs involves ruffing with an honour, and this declarer cannot afford. Turning to the diamonds, a 4-2 break is to be expected, so an over-ruff is a serious danger. Can it be circumvented? Josephine Culbertson found a neat way out. At trick two, she led the ◇3. Ruffing the spade return, she crossed to the ♡K and ruffed a low diamond, setting up the suit, despite the 4-2 break. It remained only to draw trumps, ending in dummy, and to throw four clubs on the diamonds.

'One can't do more than play with the odds,' lamented the Professor. 'Of course, had I known . . . but one can't have one's cake and eat it, too.'

'And why not?' asked the Senior Kibitzer.

Dlr. South
Love all

```
                    ♠ A Q 2
                    ♡ 7 5
                    ◇ A J 9 6 5
                    ♣ 4 3 2
    ♠ 8 7 6                        ♠ K 10 9
    ♡ K 10 9 2          N          ♡ J 8 6 4 3
    ◇ 8 4          W       E       ◇ 3
    ♣ J 10 9 8          S          ♣ Q 7 6 5
                    ♠ J 5 4 3
                    ♡ A Q
                    ◇ K Q 10 7 2
                    ♣ A K
```

South	North
1◇	3◇
3♡	3♠
6◇	

West led the ♣J. After drawing trumps, South took the losing spade finesse. East returned a heart and South was in a dilemma. Either the heart finesse or a 3-3 spade break would see him home, but he couldn't try both. The finesse being the better chance, he inserted the ♡Q and went down.

'Instead of that fatuous spade finesse,' said SK reprovingly, 'you should have played the ♠A, then the ♠2. If East produces the ♠K, there's no further problem. If your ♠J holds, you can play two more rounds of spades and find out how the land lies before staking everything on the heart finesse. The same applies if West has the ♠K, since he can't lead a heart. Either way, you can test the spades safely without giving up the heart finesse.'

'An excellent contract,' declared the Professor defiantly. 'The odds in favour . . .'

'I am sure you are right,' rejoined the Senior Kibitzer, 'but why not make the contract instead of computing the odds in its favour?'

Dlr. South
Both vul.

```
                  ♠ A 7 6 3
                  ♡ J 4
                  ◊ K 6 4 3 2
                  ♣ K 3
   ♠ Q J 9 8 2                      ♠ K 5 4
   ♡ Q 7 6 3         N              ♡ 5 2
   ◊ 8 7          W     E           ◊ Q J 10 9
   ♣ A 8             S              ♣ 7 6 5 4
                  ♠ 10
                  ♡ A K 10 9 8
                  ◊ A 5
                  ♣ Q J 10 9 2
```

South	North
1♣	1◊
1♡	2NT
3♡	4♡

West led the ♠Q. The Professor went up with the ♠A and ran the ♡J which held the trick. A second heart to the ♡10 followed. This time West won and forced declarer with a spade. The Professor laid down the ♡A and shook his head sadly when East showed out. Then he proceeded to drive out the ♣A, but another spade forced out his last trump and he ended up two down.

'What made you embark upon a trump finesse you didn't need?' asked SK. 'Couldn't you cash the ♡AK and play clubs, allowing defenders to score their two trumps, separately if the suit breaks 3-3? Either way they couldn't come to more than three tricks.

'Mind you,' added SK, 'West should have won the first heart. He gave you a second chance which you didn't deserve.'

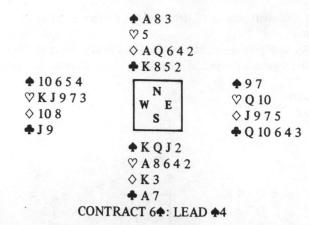

♠ A 8 3
♡ 5
◇ A Q 6 4 2
♣ K 8 5 2

♠ 10 6 5 4
♡ K J 9 7 3
◇ 10 8
♣ J 9

♠ 9 7
♡ Q 10
◇ J 9 7 5
♣ Q 10 6 4 3

♠ K Q J 2
♡ A 8 6 4 2
◇ K 3
♣ A 7

CONTRACT 6♠: LEAD ♠4

South has ten top tricks, four trumps, the ♡A, ◇AKQ and the ♣AK. Needing two more, he wins the first trick with the ♠A and sets out to ruff two hearts in dummy. This is the natural line of play and most of the time it will succeed. Occasionally, however, the distribution will be unkind, as above, and a defender will ruff the third rounds of hearts.

Unlucky? Certainly, but declarer can guard against it. Expecting the spades and diamonds to break 4-2, in accordance with the odds, he plays a low diamond from both hands at trick two. Now, unless the trumps or diamonds are 5-1, all is well. A trump return is the best defence, but it won't worry South. He wins, ruffs a heart, comes to hand with the ♣A, draws trumps, cashes the ◇K and crosses to dummy with the ♣K to score three good diamonds.

This is a hand of recent origin and declarer, a player of standing, allowed himself to be unlucky. Fifty years ago, as the first hand in this chapter shows, Josephine Culbertson would have given misfortune short shrift.

Dlr. South
Both vul.

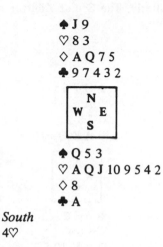

♠ J 9
♡ 8 3
◇ A Q 7 5
♣ 9 7 4 3 2

♠ Q 5 3
♡ A Q J 10 9 5 4 2
◇ 8
♣ A

South
4♡

West leads the ♣K. Assuming that there is nothing devilish about the distribution, can South make certain of his contract? How should he play?

South has four possible losers, a trump and three spades. Of course, the trump finesse may be right or West could have the ♠10 or else both the ♠A and ♠K. That presupposes a measure of luck. To succeed without it, declarer should cross to the ◇A and lead the ♠9. If East wins, it will not help him to lead a trump, for then declarer will no longer need to ruff a spade. If West wins, he cannot lead a trump without giving up a trick. Even if he started with the three outstanding trumps, it would do him no good. Declarer would lead a second spade and ruff the third one — or not lose a trick to the ♡K.

♠ A 8 6 2   ♠ K 10 7 4
♡ K 7   ♡ 6
◇ J 6 3   ◇ K 10 9 4 2
♣ K Q 10 8   ♣ J 6 5

'If I bring off a finesse, there must be something wrong somewhere,' said the Professor bitterly. The Senior Kibitzer raised a disapproving eyebrow.

Dlr. South
E/W vul.

```
                    ♠ Q 7 6 5
                    ♡ A
                    ◇ J 8 2
                    ♣ A K Q J 10
   ♠ K J 8                         ♠ 10 9 4
   ♡ K Q 10 8 6        N           ♡ 7 5 3 2
   ◇ 4            W         E      ◇ Q 9 7 6
   ♣ 7 6 4 2          S           ♣ 8 3
                    ♠ A 3 2
                    ♡ J 8 4
                    ◇ A K 10 5 3
                    ♣ 9 5
```

South	North
1◇	3♣
3◇	4◇
4♣	5♡
6◇	

West led the ♡K and the Professor smiled happily. He could afford to lose the trump finesse, so at trick two he led the ◇2 to his ◇10. Surprisingly it held. A heart ruff was going to be his twelfth trick. Now it would be the thirteenth. So he ruffed a heart and led another trump. Alas, when West showed out, the thirteen tricks shrank to eleven. He couldn't afford to give up a trump, while he still had a losing heart, so he tried to get discards on clubs, but East ruffed, and though the ♠K was right, there was a spade to lose.

'You were too lucky,' said SK scornfully. 'Had the trump finesse failed, all would have been well. Why, then, didn't you try to make it fail? At trick two you lead the ◇J, and whether or not East covers, you play low. Now you are safe.'

Dlr. North
Both Vul.

> ♠ K J 3
> ♡ 7 2
> ◇ 6 5 2
> ♣ A K Q 10 2

> ♠ A Q 10 9 8
> ♡ 8 6 4
> ◇ A 9 4 3
> ♣ J

West	North	East	South
–	1♣	1♡	1♠
2♡	2♠	Pass	4♠

West leads the ♡K, then the ♡Q. East overtakes with the ♡A and switches to the ♣9. How should South play?

When this hand came up in play, declarer took three rounds of trumps, ending in dummy, and led clubs. West ruffed the third club and South still had two losers. Two down.

♠ 7 6 5 4	N	♠ 2
♡ K Q 5	W E	♡ A J 10 9 3
◇ Q J 10 7	S	◇ K 8
♣ 4 3		♣ 9 8 7 6 5

Naturally South complained of bad luck, but he deserved no sympathy, for it required only a little care to ensure the contract.

Declarer should take two rounds of trumps only. If either defender shows out, he plays clubs, his first discard being a heart. Let West ruff. Whatever he returns, South wins, draws the last trump with dummy's ♠K – after his ruff West has one trump only left – and plays clubs, scoring five trumps, four clubs and the ◇A.

Losing with bad cards is depressing. Losing with good ones is infuriating. It's so bad for morale. So make sure of game here:

Dlr. North
Love all

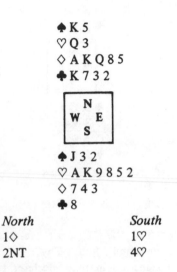

♠K 5
♡Q 3
◇A K Q 8 5
♣K 7 3 2

♠J 3 2
♡A K 9 8 5 2
◇7 4 3
♣8

North	South
1◇	1♡
2NT	4♡

West leads the ♣6. You play low from dummy and East's ♠A wins. Another spade comes back.

You can see twelve tricks, if both red suits break kindly. But then there's be no problem, so you rightly look for snags.

Since you can't afford to lose another spade, you must ruff one and you have no immediate entry to your hand. To create one, you lead a club. Whatever opponents return, you come to hand with a club ruff, ruff a spade in dummy, cash the ♡Q and get back with another club ruff.

All that remains is to lay down the ♡AK, and leaving the best trump out, cash the ◇AK.

♠Q 8 7 6
♡J 10 7 4
◇6
♣A Q 6 5

♠A 10 9 4
♡6
◇J 10 9 2
♣J 10 9 4

Easy? Perhaps, because seeing the hand as a problem, you're on your guard. But would you have played that club at the table?

Dlr. West
E/W vul.

```
              ♠ J 8 7 6
              ♡ 8 5 4
              ◇ A Q
              ♣ K Q J 5

                  N
              W       E
                  S

              ♠ A K 4 3 2
              ♡ A K
              ◇ 8 6
              ♣ A 10 3 2
```

North	*South*
1♣	2♠
3♠	4♣
4◇	4♡
4♠	5♡
5♠	6♠

West leads the ♡Q. How should declarer play?

The key to the hand lies in the diamond finesse, so at trick two declarer should forthwith put it to the test.

If the finesse loses, he must lead out his ♠AK, hoping to drop the ♠Q in two rounds. There's no other hope.

If the diamond finesse succeeds, the contract is safe — so long as declarer makes certain that he doesn't lose more than one trick in trumps.

At trick three he leads the ♠6 and runs it unless East covers. This is a Safety Play against ♠Q1095 with East, the only distribution which can endanger the contract.

```
  ♠ —                        ♠ Q 10 9 5
  ♡ Q J 10 9        N        ♡ 7 6 3 2
  ◇ K J 9 7 5 2   W   E      ◇ 10 4 3
  ♣ 9 8 7            S        ♣ 6 4
```

Experts know most of the standard Safety Plays by heart, but anybody can get there on the spot simply by visualising the most unfavourable distribution.

'Everything wrong, as usual,' exclaimed the Professor bitterly.
'Including the play,' murmured the Senior Kibitzer.

Dlr. South
N/S vul.

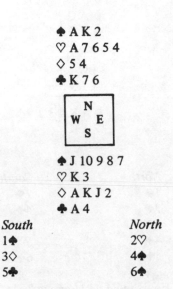

♠ A K 2
♡ A 7 6 5 4
◇ 5 4
♣ K 7 6

♠ J 10 9 8 7
♡ K 3
◇ A K J 2
♣ A 4

South	North
1♠	2♡
3◇	4♠
5♣	6♠

West led the ♣10. Winning in his hand, the Professor decided to test the
hearts. If they were 3-3, he could spread his hand.

If they broke 4-2, one long heart and a diamond ruff should ensure
the contract. After the ♡K, the ♡A and a heart ruff, East shedding a
diamond, he crossed to the ♠K and ruffed another heart. Next he led
a trump to dummy's ♠A. Alas, West showed out and the hand collapsed.

♠ 4
♡ Q 10 9 8
◇ Q 10 7 6 3
♣ 10 9 8

♠ Q 6 5 3
♡ J 2
◇ 9 8
♣ Q J 5 3 2

'The diamond finesse was wrong, too,' began the Professor, 'so . . .'
'So there was no need to take it, or to touch hearts,' rejoined SK.
'All you had to do was to win the first trick in dummy, cash the ◇AK
and ruff a diamond high. Getting back with the ♡K you would ruff
your last diamond with dummy's second honour and exit with a trump.

Someone should write a treatise on how not to finesse. Today's hand is an example constructed by W.H. Kelsey.

Dlr. South
Both vul.

```
                   ♠ A J 10 9
                   ♡ 9 7 6 4
                   ◇ 8 6
                   ♣ J 5 2
  ♠ K 8 3                          ♠ 7 6 2
  ♡ J 8 5 2        ┌─────┐         ♡ Q 10 3
  ◇ A 10 7 5 3     │  N  │         ◇ J 9 2
  ♣ 4              │W   E│         ♣ K 8 7 3
                   │  S  │
                   └─────┘
                   ♠ Q 5 4
                   ♡ A K
                   ◇ K Q 4
                   ♣ A Q 10 9 6
         South                North
         2NT                  3♣
         3NT
```

West leads the ◇5 to the ◇J and ◇K.

The inexperienced South takes the spade finesse, then the club finesse and makes twelve tricks.

The expert realises that he needs only the club finesse, so he avoids the risk of losing the lead to East. Besides, if West has the ♠K, he is safe anyway. Like the novice, he leads the ♠Q, but regardless of West's card, he goes up with the ♠A. The ♣J is followed by the ♣2, revealing the 4-1 split. So the finesse must be repeated and West has to have the ♠K after all. The unblocking play of the ♠Q at trick two now brings its rewards. Had declarer led a low spade to the ♠A, West would hold up his ♠K and there would be no second entry to dummy.

'Surely partner,' said the Professor accusingly, 'with all those key cards, you should have called the grand slam.'

Dlr. North
Love all

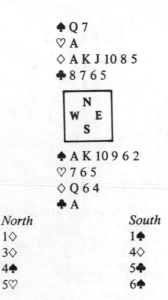

        ♠ Q 7
        ♡ A
        ◇ A K J 10 8 5
        ♣ 8 7 6 5

        ♠ A K 10 9 6 2
        ♡ 7 6 5
        ◇ Q 6 4
        ♣ A

North	*South*
1◇	1♠
3◇	4◇
4♣	5♣
5♡	6♠

West led the ♡K and, counting aloud, the Professor listed fourteen tricks – six spades, six diamonds and two aces.

'Yes,' agreed the Senior Kibitzer, 'it's simple enough in a grand slam. Now in six . . .'

The Professor played the ♠Q, then the ♠7. East showed out and the fourteen tricks quickly shrank to ten, for the defence couldn't be denied two hearts and a trump.

♠ J 8 5 4   ♠ 3
♡ K Q 10 8 4   N   ♡ J 9 3 2
◇ 3   W   E   ◇ 9 7 2
♣ J 10 9   S   ♣ K Q 4 3 2

'Since you had to make twelve tricks, not fourteen,' observed SK drily, 'you might have considered the one and only danger, a 4-1 trump break. To guard against it you would have led the ♠7 and finessed. You could afford to lose the trick, for the ♠Q would still be there to deal with a heart return, and no matter what West played, you would make the rest.'

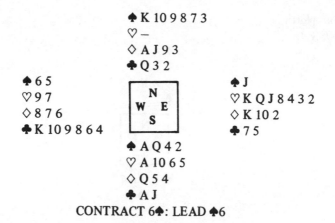

♠ K 10 9 8 7 3
♡ –
◇ A J 9 3
♣ Q 3 2

♠ 6 5
♡ 9 7
◇ 8 7 6
♣ K 10 9 8 6 4

♠ J
♡ K Q J 8 4 3 2
◇ K 10 2
♣ 7 5

♠ A Q 4 2
♡ A 10 6 5
◇ Q 5 4
♣ A J

CONTRACT 6♠: LEAD ♠6

Declarer wins trick one in his hand. How should he play?

When this hand came up at the St James's Bridge Club in London declarer went down. British international Claude Rodrigue, a spectator deputising for the Senior Kibitzer, reports a long and spirited argument about the merits of taking the diamond finesse before the club finesse and *vice versa*.

The odds are long in declarer's favour — so long as he takes neither. If the diamond finesse loses and a club comes back, declarer won't know what to do. Should he finesse or hope for a 3-3 diamond break or for the ◇10 to come down? He must guess.

The answer is to lead the ◇3. If East has the ◇K, there's no further problem. Either he goes up and the ♣J can be discarded on dummy's ◇J or he plays low, allowing declarer to give up a club.

Should West turn up with the ◇K, declarer will have time to test the diamond break. If need be, he will later take the club finesse. He will have given himself every chance, without having to guess anything.

Dlr. North
N/S vul.

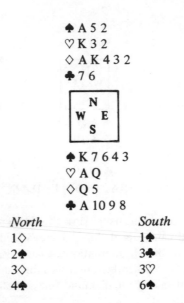

♠ A 5 2
♡ K 3 2
◇ A K 4 3 2
♣ 7 6

♠ K 7 6 4 3
♡ A Q
◇ Q 5
♣ A 10 9 8

North	South
1◇	1♠
2♠	3♣
3◇	3♡
4♣	6♠

The bidding is venturesome, to say the least, but West doesn't find the killing club opening and on the lead of the ♡J the contract isn't unreasonable. How should South play to give himself the best chance?

Trumps must break 3-2 or there's no hope. If the diamonds split 3-3, all is well, but that's too much to expect. Declarer can greatly improve his chances by taking two rounds of diamonds and ruffing a diamond, before touching trumps. Again, if the diamonds are 3-3, there's no problem, but now declarer brings home his contract even if they are 4-2, so long as the defender who is short in diamonds has the three trumps.

♠ Q 10 9
♡ J 10 9 8
◇ 7 6
♣ K J 3 2

♠ J 8
♡ 7 6 5 4
◇ J 10 9 8
♣ Q 5 4

If West over-ruffs, the ♠5 is an entry to the long diamond. If he doesn't, South takes two rounds of trumps, ending in dummy, and leads diamonds discarding clubs till West ruffs.

Dlr. South
Love all

```
              ♠ 10 9 6 4
              ♡ K 7
              ◇ A 8 3 2
              ♣ A 5 4
              ┌─────────┐
              │    N    │
              │ W     E │
              │    S    │
              └─────────┘
              ♠ 8
              ♡ A Q J 9 4
              ◇ Q J 10 6
              ♣ K Q J
```

South	West	North	East
1♡	1♠	2◇	Pass
3◇	Pass	3♡	Pass
4♡			

West leads the ♠K and ♠Q, East following with the ♠2, then the ♠3. How should South play in 6♡?

Unless there's something diabolical afoot, the game is in no danger. West should have the ◇K for his bid, and if so, declarer will make his slam, too — but only if he has bid it.

What if he hasn't?

Most of the time the inexperienced player will still make twelve tricks. Occasionally, however, East will turn up unexpectedly with the ◇K and trumps will break 4-2. Then he will go down.

Having stopped in 4♡, the expert won't make twelve tricks, even if they are there. Visualising this distribution:

```
  ♠ A K Q J 5      ┌─────────┐    ♠ 7 3 2
  ♡ 10 6 3 2       │    N    │    ♡ 8 5
  ◇ 9 4            │ W     E │    ◇ K 7 5
  ♣ 8 7            │    S    │    ♣ 10 9 6 3 2
                   └─────────┘
```

he will discard a diamond on the second spade, ruff a third one and draw trumps, leaving himself with none. Now, however, finding East with the ◇K will present no danger for he will have no spade left.

'A void in one hand, a singleton in the other and a finesse wrong into the bargain,' lamented the Professor. 'The odds against it must be . . .'

'Very likely,' rejoined the Senior Kibitzer, 'but since the contract is unbreakable, why worry about odds?'

Dlr. North
Both vul.

```
                    ♠ J
                    ♡ 8 4 3
                    ◇ K Q J 10 9
                    ♣ 7 6 5 3
   ♠ A K 9 4 2                        ♠ Q 10 7 6 5
   ♡ 7 6 5           N                ♡ —
   ◇ 2           W       E            ◇ A 7 6 5 4 3
   ♣ K J 9 4         S                ♣ 10 8
                    ♠ 8 3
                    ♡ A K Q J 10 9 2
                    ◇ 8
                    ♣ A Q 2
```

West	North	East	South
–	Pass	Pass	4♡

The Professor agreed later that he was too good to pre-empt with 4♡, but his luck being what it was, he wanted to make sure of the rubber.

West began with the two top spades. The Professor ruffed in dummy, laid down the ♡A and continued with the ◇8. Winning with the ◇A, East returned a club. The Professor went up with the ♣A and crossing to dummy's ♡8, tried to cash the ◇Q for his tenth trick. West, however, ruffed and exited with his third trump.

'Why didn't you allow West to hold the second trick?' asked SK reproachfully. 'Whatever he played next, you would drive out the ◇A, draw trumps, ending with the ♡8 in dummy, and claim the rest. Now had West led a *low* spade at trick two . . .'

'Why do my partners play so badly?' said South to his Guardian Angel. 'Other people's partners do the right thing, even when it's wrong. Why . . .'

The G.A. waved his magic wand.

Dlr. South
N/S game

```
              ♠ 2
              ♡ 10 6 5 4 2
              ◇ A Q J 3 2
              ♣ K 5

              ┌─────────┐
              │    N    │
              │ W     E │
              │    S    │
              └─────────┘

              ♠ A K 10
              ♡ K Q 3
              ◇ 10 6 5
              ♣ A 7 4 2
```

South	North
1♣	1♡
1NT	3◇
3♡	3NT

West led the ♠5 to East's ♠Q and South's ♠K. South looked up reproachfully at his G.A. Why hadn't North bid 4♡?

The ◇10 lost to East's ◇K and the ♠9 came back. West captured the ♠10 with the ♠J and cleared the suit. South had only eight tricks and West, unluckily, had an entry with the ♡A.

'Why . . .' began South, and then he saw the light. He didn't need the diamond finesse. He should have gone up with the ◇A and led a heart. If East had the ♡A, a 3-2 heart break would have sufficed. Had West the ♡A, he could do no harm and South would set up the diamonds.

```
♠ J 8 6 5 4 3      ┌─────────┐      ♠ Q 9 7
♡ A J 9 8 7        │    N    │      ♡ —
◇ 4                │ W     E │      ◇ K 9 8 7
♣ Q                │    S    │      ♣ J 10 9 8 6 3
                   └─────────┘
```

North did the wrong thing at the right time. South, alas, failed him.

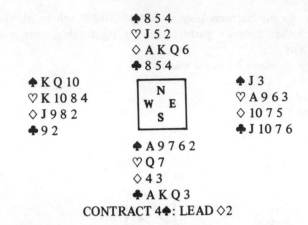

```
                    ♠ 8 5 4
                    ♡ J 5 2
                    ◇ A K Q 6
                    ♣ 8 5 4
      ♠ K Q 10                        ♠ J 3
      ♡ K 10 8 4        N             ♡ A 9 6 3
      ◇ J 9 8 2     W       E         ◇ 10 7 5
      ♣ 9 2              S            ♣ J 10 7 6
                    ♠ A 9 7 6 2
                    ♡ Q 7
                    ◇ 4 3
                    ♣ A K Q 3
```

CONTRACT 4♠: LEAD ◇2

A lucky lead. How should declarer play?

After discarding a heart on dummy's third top diamond, South has three losers, a heart and two trumps. To allow for the likely 4-2 club break, he must duck a round of trumps, then lay down the ace and play clubs, ready to ruff one, if necessary. If a club is ruffed or over-ruffed by a defender, it will be with the master trump, so South won't mind.

When this hand came up, declarer, Blue Team star Mimo d'Alelio, foresaw what might happen. The same defender might have three trumps and four diamonds, as above. Winning the first trump, he would lead the diamond for his partner to ruff, 'uppercutting' South's ace.

To guard against this defence d'Alelio played dummy's fourth diamond and discarded his second heart, exchanging one loser for another. No longer threatened by an uppercut, he could now afford to duck a round of trumps.